the
Best is Yet
To Come

FRAN FERNANDEZ

the *Best is Yet To Come*

~ 60 DEVOTIONS ~

ZONDERVAN®

ZONDERVAN.com/
AUTHORTRACKER
follow your favorite authors

ZONDERVAN

The Best Is Yet to Come: 60 Devotions
Copyright © 2009 by Fran Fernandez

Requests for information should be addressed to:

Zondervan, *Grand Rapids, Michigan* 49530

Library of Congress Cataloging-in-Publication Data

Fernandez, Fran, 1942–
    The best is yet to come: 60 devotions / Fran Fernandez.
       p. cm.
    Includes bibliographical references and index.
    ISBN 978-0-310-28753-7 (hardcover, jacketed: alk. paper)
    1. Christian women—Prayers and devotions. I. Title.
  BV4844.F47 2009
  242'.643—dc22
                                           2008040331

Published in association with Hartline Literary Agency, Pittsburgh, Pennsylvania 15235.

Interior design by Christine Orejuela-Winkelman

Printed in the United States of America

09 10 11 12 13 14 • 22 21 20 19 18 17 16 15 14 13 12 11 10 9 8 7 6 5 4 3 2 1

Contents

Acknowledgments

The single greatest thing I have ever done is to say *yes* to Jesus Christ's gift of salvation. The Lord gave me the desire to write and then opened the way—it is to Him I dedicate this book.

The second greatest thing was to say *yes* to Frank, my faithful hubby of forty-six years, who has shown me an earthly picture of the patience and love of the Lord.

From the germ of a yearning to write over forty-five years ago, Frank, along with my sister Angela (and after she married, her hubby Steve), were my first cheering team. In the early 1970s Angela gave me *The Nothing Book* and told me to fill it up, and that one day I would have a book with my name on it—and here it is!

Then along came Sue, my dearest friend who encouraged me while teaching me basics of good English grammar. Eventually, my three gifts from God (our children),

Frank, Maria Elena, and John, grew up and joined the cheering team. With their spouses, Carolyn, Chris, and Holly, they've given me the world's grandest grandchildren: Laura, Jackie, J. C., Julia, Christine, Frankie, and the twins, Zach and Maddie. Now I have a stadium section full of inspiration and joy!

God's blessings abound through them, the friends, and the church family He has graciously given me. One of the blessings of this book being published has been seeing the joy that others have for me. I love and thank each of you—for your fellowship in the gospel, for your encouragement, and for your faithful prayers. God bless you all.

Thanks are also due to my agent, Tamela Hancock Murray, who helped make this possible with her expertise and encouragement. Thank you.

I'd be remiss if I didn't thank my editor, Sue Brower, who has shown me that a good editor is indeed a gift from God, one much like a dedicated orchestra conductor, who directs with expertise and encouragement, guiding a writer to fine-tune her work, and hopefully making it sing for Him.

Last, but not at all least, I thank Patti Souder, the tireless director of Montrose Christian Writers Conference of Montrose, PA. It was there this book started. Patti, and her wonderful faculty, and all the great fellow conferees have for years been coaches, encouragers, and a shining model of Christian writers' camaraderie. Thank you all!

Preface

For over thirty-eight years the Lord has been faithful to me. He has loved me when I have been less than lovable. He has been patient and forgiving when I have not been. His word has been my anchor, my lighthouse, and my rock. Through His unconditional love and everlasting, living Word, I have grown to know and love Him more and more. I have come to realize there is nothing, there is no one, to compare. He is the lover of my soul, He calls me His beloved, He tells me I am His delight. He whispers daily for me to come into His inner chamber, sit on His lap, put my head on His chest, and listen to His heartbeat of love for me. Soaking in His beauty and the glory of His presence, every day is an adventure—and with Him, the best is always yet to come!

Prayerfully, what has been written will inspire you to daily press in for more of Him, that you will take this book and the Word in hand and go with great anticipation of heart to the place where He is and be filled to overflowing with that for which you were created—Him. It is for this that I wrote the book.

Taking Your Mountains

WITH YOUR HELP I CAN ADVANCE AGAINST A TROOP;
WITH MY GOD I CAN SCALE A WALL.

Psalm 18:29

The average woman is usually not too interested in mountain climbing (though it is a great experience). Nevertheless, God calls us to be mountain takers, whatever our age.

For forty-five years Caleb served with Moses in the wilderness—and that was just the warm-up for taking his mountain.

Caleb was a man of God who saw a mountain as a challenge. Instead of thinking he was too old at eighty-five, he said he was as strong as when he was forty. And then Caleb declared that with the Lord's help, he'd take that mountain ... and he started climbing (Joshua 14:10–15).

Winston Churchill didn't see his older years as a time to go around the mountain, or to retire. He became prime minister of England at sixty-two years old. His greatest contribution came as a senior. Not only was he blessed, but the entire free world was blessed by Churchill's leadership.

You are not Caleb, and you're not Winston Churchill, but you are the unique *you*, with gifts and talents from God for your world today.

Imagination is a wonderful thing. What is it you'd do for God if there were no barriers? Whatever it is — He tells us we can do more even than that!

Eva Marie Everson's[1] career and ministry began when she was over the hill. One day a friend asked Eva what she'd want to do for the Lord if she could do anything. "Write and speak," Eva replied.[2]

Well — Eva's now an award-winning author, co-author, international speaker, journalist, seminary graduate, and mentor with the Christian Writers Guild, among other things. How? Because she had faith that God put the desire in her heart, and that He'd bring it to pass if she'd start hiking (Philippians 2:13).

Eva saw her mountain as a challenge and not a stop sign.

Holding God's guiding hand, Eva began to scale the mountain one step at a time. And she's still climbing, with no signs of stopping. If you listen, you might hear her singing, "Ain't no mountain high enough, Ain't no valley low enough" … to keep me from following His dream for me.

There are many mountains yet to be scaled, beckoning for you to come and dream big. God says, "Now to him who is able to do immeasurably more than all we ask or imagine, according to his power that is at work within us (Ephesians 3:20).

Let's be like Caleb and Eva, who were too busy climbing to worry about growing older. Each day look for a new mountain to take for the kingdom, and you'll forge a blazing trail for younger Christians to follow.

Being a mature Christian woman just means we're that much closer to the summit. Meanwhile, let's get out our hiking boots and start climbing!

PRAYER: *Oh, Lord, may I look for fresh ways to serve You. Open my eyes to the talents and gifts You have given me for Your use. Help me see how I can use them for Your glory. Let me not limit You, for I know with You all things are possible. Let me take the mountains You have set before me and then look for another one. Open my eyes, Lord. Amen.*

Make it yours: Take a minute and dream with God. What is some mountain you'd like to take? Nothing is impossible with you and God. Daydream on paper: write down what you would do for God if there were no limitations. Then after you decide on just one thing, give it to God. Think about and write down: what is one small thing you can do to plan toward climbing that mountain. Then put on your hiking boots and do it!

God, Can You Help Me?

AND I WILL ASK THE FATHER, AND HE WILL GIVE YOU
ANOTHER COUNSELOR [HELPER] TO BE WITH YOU FOREVER.

John 14:16

Everybody needs help once in a while. It can seem, with the passing of years, that we need it more often. Perhaps as we mature we naturally tend to pick up more responsibilities—or maybe they just find us.

Either way, we are not alone. Jesus promised that when He left this earth, He'd send us a Helper in His place—the Holy Spirit. Jesus Himself knew what it was to need help. He can empathize when we are troubled and need to be upheld.

In the garden of Gethsemane when Jesus' soul was troubled and deeply distressed, God sent an angel to strengthen Him (Luke 22:43). Jesus had those dearest to Him forsake and not understand Him or His mission.

Maybe you are going through a hard time and wonder how you're going to make it over the finish line. Bills overdue, broken relationships, a daunting project … maybe your kids are coming back home after they left the nest, or maybe you are now the constant caretaker for parents. Take heart, for God has sent the Helper to come alongside to make sure you finish.

Derek Redmond, the English athlete, knows what that kind of help is like. He was determined to win a medal in the 400 meter race at the 1992 Olympics in Barcelona, Spain. Derek's father had accompanied him, as he did for all the world competitions. It was his father, Jim, who ran right alongside Derek when he was training.

At 175 meters from the finish line, Redmond was well in the lead, a sure winner. Suddenly, he was on the ground in great pain; he had popped his right hamstring. The medics ran with the stretcher, but he refused it. Struggling to get up, he told them he was going to finish. Sixty-five thousand people stood in disbelief and roared in encouragement and support. Slowly, Derek Redmond took one agonizing step after another.

Derek's father leaped over the railing, barely avoiding two security guards chasing him. He ran to Derek's side yelling that it was his son, and he was going to help him finish the race. Jim Redmond wrapped his arm around Derek's waist and told him that they'd finish together.

Arm in arm, they made it up to the finish line. Jim

released his hold on Derek so that he'd make it over the finish line by himself.

The headlines that day read: Derek and dad finish Olympic 400 together.[1]

This is a vivid picture of the Helper we have in the Holy Spirit. He comes alongside and He helps us in whatever way is needed. That's His job. And if we can't make it over the finish line, He'll carry us!

PRAYER: *Thank You for sending me the Holy Spirit to help me in all things. May I turn to Him often, seeking His wisdom, guidance, and comfort. Let me rejoice that You will never leave me or forsake me. Whatever is on my plate today, I know You and I can do it together; if not, You'll carry me. Thank you.*

Make it yours: Change the title of today's devotion—*God Can You Help Me?*—to read instead, *God, You Can Help Me!* Say it out loud with feeling, knowing God can and will help you always.

Come Away My Beloved

My lover spoke and said to me, "Arise, my darling,
my beautiful one, and come with me."
Song of Songs 2:10

The Lord has put in each of our spirits the ability to hear and to respond to His call. When we respond, it will very much be for our good and for our greatest pleasure and enjoyment.

At times, we can become so accustomed to sounds, such as dinner music in a restaurant or a radio playing in the background at home, that we can miss the latest news or a new song.

The cares and busyness of life can dull our hearts and ears, leaving us insensitive to His call. If this happens, we will miss one of the great joys of the Christian life—hearing and fellowshipping with God.

David was a man after God's own heart. He not only

heard, but responded, to the voice of His Lord. David knew it was in the secret place where he'd meet with God and have the joy of intimate communion.

"One thing I ask of the LORD, this is what I seek: that I may dwell in the house of the LORD all the days of my life, to gaze upon the beauty of the LORD and to seek Him in his temple" (Psalm 27:4).

When a loved one has gone on a trip and tells you they're finally coming home Tuesday evening, how much more intently do you listen for the car in the driveway? Cars passing by your house on previous days went unnoticed. However, now you're aware of each passing car. Why? Because you are listening and expecting.

When Samuel was a boy, he didn't know that God spoke to His people. Therefore, when God spoke to him, Samuel thought it was Eli the high priest calling him. Eli told Samuel it was God, and that Samuel should say the next time God called, "Speak, for your servant is listening" (1 Samuel 3:10).

Before you begin your day, seek after the beautiful one. As you climb on His lap and open your ear, you'll hear Him whispering that you are His darling and His beautiful one—come and enjoy Him! What a way to start a day!

And, if you have to jump out of bed and hit the floor running once in awhile, let these words ring in your ears throughout your race, "Arise, my darling, my beautiful one," I am with you (Song of Songs 2:10).

PRAYER: *Oh Lord, thank You for loving me, and calling me to come. May I truly know and believe that Your desire is for me, that I am Your darling and Your beautiful one. You are my beautiful one. Open my ears so I may hear Your call. Amen.*

Make it yours: Come to the Lord with the purpose to hear His voice calling you. With the Word in hand, follow David and Samuel's example by actively seeking and listening. Tell God, "I will seek your face, I will listen—speak Lord, speak." Then expect to hear Him.

Fear of Daying

SO DO NOT FEAR, FOR I AM WITH YOU; DO NOT BE DISMAYED,
FOR I AM YOUR GOD. I WILL STRENGTHEN YOU AND HELP YOU;
I WILL UPHOLD YOU WITH MY RIGHTEOUS RIGHT HAND.

Isaiah 41:10

A wonderful truth of our Christian faith is we are set free from fear of dying. However, at times, it's the day-to-day living that will bring us tension and anxiety if we let it.

I know. I have faced the real possibility of dying. I'm happy to say it wasn't the dying that gripped me. I found I was indeed set free from fear of death through God's Word and His grace.

Keying away on the computer one day, I intended to write, *as Christians we are set free from fear of dying.* Instead, I mistakenly keyed in that we were set free from fear of *daying.* I looked at it, and inwardly smiled—how true it was. Dying, I can handle. *Daying* sometimes I can't.

While all days do not start or end the same, they all hold the same promise of His presence. God has said there is not a day or a night that He will not be there to help and strengthen. Every moment His hand is there to uphold; our part is to fear not, and not be dismayed. How can we do this in the face of seemingly impossible situations? It is by faith in God and His Word; He is our God, He is with us—and God doesn't lie.

We may start our day with a preplanned agenda and our to-do list, thinking we have everything taken care of for the most part. Whether we are forty, fifty, or sixty and still counting, we like to think we have our days pretty much under control. The fact is, we never can tell what might be waiting ahead for us. But, the good news is, God is never taken by surprise, and He is always with us.

One ordinary day, an ordinary teenage boy, David, was sent to see how his brothers were faring in the war camp. He knew not what awaited him that day. But, he knew His God. He had tested Him throughout His life and had found God faithful for anything a day could bring. This day, it was a towering giant.

His brothers, the soldiers, and even King Saul feared that day—but not David. He had no fear of *daying*, for David came to Goliath in the name of the Lord—and we know by the end of the day, David had won and Goliath was dead at his feet.

"The LORD who delivered me from the paw of the

lion and the paw of the bear will deliver me from the hand of this Philistine" (1 Samuel 17:37).

None of us will face an actual giant any time soon. But, we all will face a day, or perhaps days, filled with knowns and unknowns that can make us fearful. It is then we have to know that He is with us, and He will help us. Remember, He has never failed you yet.

> **PRAYER:** *Dear Lord, thank You that You are a faithful and powerful God. There is not a day that will come that I need to fear what it will bring, for You are with me and will uphold me by your right hand. Amen.*

Make it yours: Write down Isaiah 41:10 and read it out loud. Meditate word by word, phrase by phrase as you begin to memorize it today.

Can't Wait to See the King

WHEN HE SAW QUEEN ESTHER STANDING IN THE COURT,
HE WAS PLEASED WITH HER AND HELD OUT TO HER THE GOLD
SCEPTER THAT WAS IN HIS HAND. SO ESTHER
APPROACHED AND TOUCHED THE TIP OF THE SCEPTER.

Esther 5:2

I looked out the window, daydreaming as I rode the Long Island Railroad. As the train pulled into a station, a familiar yellow and black billboard caught my eye—it was the ad for *Lion King*. It boldly proclaimed, "Can't Wait to See the King."

My thoughts then wandered from *Lion King* to the King of Kings. How much more can we be excited to see our King, Jesus Christ? We are the ones who should be shouting from the roof tops, "Can't wait to see the King!"

And to see Him, we don't have to order tickets in

advance; we don't have to hope to get good seats. Nor do we have to take a train or a bus, and then have to wait in line worrying whether we will get in or if we still have the tickets.

In the days of Queen Esther, even as the king's wife, she could not freely enter his inner chamber. If she went in unbidden by him, and his scepter was not put forth, she would have paid with her life (Esther 4:11).

Not so with our King. His scepter is always down. We don't need a special engraved invitation. He looks for us to come. He bids us come.

Not everyone has free access to the president of the United States either—but those who are his family do. We see this truth in the familiar picture of President John F. Kennedy, where he is seated at his desk in the White House oval office. In the photo, under his desk sits John-John playing. Why was John-John allowed there? Because he was the president's son. John-John had the ear and the heart of the president of the great United States of America because he was his child. Our Father is greater than any president or king, and He desires that we come anytime, night or day, into His presence. His door is always open, and the scepter is always down. At Calvary, the temple veil was torn in two—symbolic of the great truth that by Christ Jesus the entrance into the Holy of Holies was made.

He did it for you and for me.

"For through him we both have access to the Father by one Spirit" (Ephesians 2:18).

Stop—be still—listen—and you can hear Him whisper, "Come, the door is open, my hand is out, and my heart is waiting for you. Come on in." If you look up, you'll see the light is in the window for you.

PRAYER: *Oh, Lord, how awesome is the fact that Your door is always open. I believe that Your desire is for me, for You said so. Help me, God, to have my heart always sing, I can't wait to see my King. You have bid me come, and I have come. I sit and wait and look to You. Fill me, cleanse me, and may we enjoy each other this moment. Amen.*

Make it yours: Take a moment now to enjoy the closeness of God's presence. Tell Him how happy you are you can come to Him at anytime, and that He is always waiting. Make a commitment to be there each day to spend time with your King.

Spiritual Spa Break
for the Soul

COME TO ME, ALL YOU WHO ARE WEARY AND BURDENED,
AND I WILL GIVE YOU REST. TAKE MY YOKE UPON YOU
AND LEARN FROM ME, FOR I AM GENTLE
AND HUMBLE IN HEART, AND YOU WILL FIND REST FOR YOUR
SOULS. FOR MY YOKE IS EASY AND MY BURDEN IS LIGHT.
Matthew 11:28 – 30

There are days that the minute our feet hit the floor, responsibilities are already calling—do this, finish that, go here, etc.—and each one wants first priority! We are hard taskmasters at times. We can beat ourselves up for not accomplishing everything, and then we can mull over how what we did finish could have been done better or sooner.

Talk about guilt—sometimes we are experts at it!

We need to slow down and take a breath. It's then that we can hear God whispering, "Come, and rest your soul."

Our peace is not dependent on if we have control of our life, but on *who* is in control.

Martha and Mary can vouch that stress is not just a modern dilemma (Luke 10:38–42). When Jesus was a guest in their home, Mary sat at His feet to listen, and Martha busied herself with preparations. Finally, Martha complained to Jesus that Mary wasn't helping. However, Jesus didn't respond as Martha expected.

In fact, He said Mary had chosen the better part: resting at His feet and desiring to hear His words.

Jesus rebuked Martha because her service had distracted her from Him. Serving wasn't Martha's problem, her distraction was.

It is the same for us today when we attempt by ourselves to carry, pull, and push our burdens. It is then we can take the fast road to self-induced stress. Jesus is our rest in the storm—it's in Him, and Him alone, we find our peace and joy—especially in the midst of daily pressures.

When things are going smoothly (which does happen occasionally) it's easy to have peace. However, we most want/need peace when life spins into fast-forward. It's then we could use a spiritual spa break for our world-weary soul.

A massage in the midst of a hectic day would do wonders (we can dream). My granddaughter, Jackie, is notorious for bribing anyone for a massage. She'll plop on your lap like a cat and whine until she gets one. Looking at Jackie during her massage, she reminds you of a cat outstretched in the warm sun for a nap. You couldn't get a care to stick to Jackie if you duct taped it twice over.

Daily, we need a heavenly spa break with Jesus; He is our oasis of rest. Though we see no end in sight, we climb on His lap and lay down our burdens. Looking at Him, we can only praise and thank Him for all He is. He then saturates our life-battered soul with His soothing, healing balm and covers us in heaven's fragrant oil. We leave His presence better than having spent a month at a California spa!

Remember—we can allow *our burdens* to be our master, or we can allow *our Master* to carry our burdens.

PRAYER: *Thank You Lord for the rest I have in You. Let me hear Your call to come and refuel at your feet. Help me come often to You and Your Word to refresh my weary soul. Amen.*

Make it yours: Put your name in place of *you* and *your* in today's verse, and then read it out loud.

Fountain of Youth

How beautiful you are, my darling!
Oh, how beautiful! Your eyes are doves.

Song of Songs 1:15

The Spanish explorer Ponce de Leon, on hearsay alone, set out to discover the fountain of eternal youth. He may be gone—but his quest is alive and well today. Many hearts still beat with the same dream to stay young longer—yes, even some of us mature Christians.

Women will go to great lengths with the hope to reverse, hold off, or at least to disguise the ravages of time. People spend billions each year to look younger—for just awhile longer.

In a world that worships youth and beauty, sometimes it's hard to see aging from God's perspective. Getting older may indeed include wrinkles, dimmer eyesight, and wider girth. But, we can see them as evidence for a life well lived for God—with its accompanying wisdom.

One of the first contacts I had with Christianity was with a den leader of the Cub Scouts. I knew something was different about her the first time I met her—it showed in her face. It wasn't her beauty (though she was attractive). It was her radiant face that spoke of a sweetness and a peace I had never seen before. I longed to have it for myself. I later found out she was a Christian.

Who, more than a Christian woman, should look and be the best she can for the kingdom? However, let us always know that our true beauty is of the heart. Inward beauty doesn't happen at a gym or a spa, and we don't even have to diet to get it. Now that's good news!

It happens at His feet with the Word, soaking up His glory. When we leave filled with His fragrance, we can diffuse it everywhere our feet carry us. We'll be a heavenly automatic air freshener! The more time we spend with Him, the more divine we are. It's this loveliness of Christ that draws others to Him.

This splendor of the Lord won't be washed away by the never ending tide of time. We'll just keep on becoming more and more like Him, until we see Him face to face, and forever we shall be like Him—beautiful (1 John 3:2).

PRAYER: *Oh, Lord, help me not be overtaken by the world's thoughts of beauty. Help me look to You and Your Word for my standard of beauty. Let me realize I am beautiful, and I am loved because I am Yours.*

Thank You that I am not cherished by You for what I look like. Help me to accept what I am and how I look, for I am made in Your image—and that's true beauty. Reveal Your tailor-made-just-for-me plan for fitness and health to serve You, to enjoy life, and to serve others. Amen.

Make it yours: When you look in the mirror today, tell yourself that you are beautiful and you are special because you are God's child. Tell someone today that God and you think she is beautiful, and let her know why. Take a paper and write down whatever time you took today for your body/beauty care routine. Give God equal time tomorrow at His feet and in His Word. This spiritual spa time will make you beautiful from the inside out—all day.

Made-to-Fit Strength

AND YOUR STRENGTH WILL EQUAL YOUR DAYS.

Deuteronomy 33:25

Have you ever wondered if you'd make it through the day when you weren't even out of bed yet? Some of us can even manage to start worrying the night before. At some point in our lives, most of us will struggle with anxiety.

It is a part of human nature to worry. That is why God has so many strong promises for us. As women, no matter what our age, no matter what our marital or financial status, there are always things we can find to worry about. (Or do they find us?)

Perhaps for you today it is a pending phone call, a difficult meeting, a doctor's report, a financial crisis. Maybe you have to get somewhere important, and are not sure how to get there. Some days just seem to greet you with a crisis tag attached.

Then, there are the life situations that don't dawn with a one-day-only expiration. You will wake up the next day and it's waiting: a recent death, a broken marriage, a severed relationship, a move, a sickness, a financial loss, or unemployment. These can not only drain our strength but ensnare us in tentacles of fear and worry if we let them.

A fact of life doesn't have to hold you prisoner. God has given us what we need to make it through life—strength for one day at a time. God promised the Israelites that their shoes wouldn't wear out—shoes made not only for walking, but climbing and fighting. On top of that, God said that whatever their day would bring, be it ease or strife, they would have enough strength (Deuteronomy 33:25).

I know. One day, after having taken some seemingly routine tests, I received an unexpected call from my doctor. I had cancer; it was in three places in my liver, and I needed to go immediately for more testing. I was home alone, and I had to give a Bible study in three hours.

I sat down on the stairs with my Bible in hand and cried out to God, "I need strength to get through these next hours … help me … I can't do this."

When my eyes went down to the open page in my lap, God answered me loud and clear: "The LORD is my strength and my song; he has become my salvation" (Psalm 118:14).

God gave me a song of faith, and I was able to get

through supper and Bible study with renewed strength, knowing that He, not me, was the source of my strength.

God gave me the strength and grace not only for the night, but for the weeks ahead, until I was blessed with the report that the cancer was gone. (Even the skeptical doctor had to admit it was a miracle.) If I had not been healed, as not all are, God's strength would have been enough for me, and for you, one day at a time.

We don't know what's hidden within the minutes of any day. Nonetheless, it is enough to know God's strength will carry us through—with an added promise of a refill for tomorrow. For when it is tomorrow, it will be our today.

PRAYER: *Thank You Lord that while I don't always know what my day holds, I do know You. Help me believe that Your many promises of strength are mine and that You are always with me. May I know that my day and my needs will never outstretch Your enduring promises of strength and provision. Thank You. Amen.*

Make it yours: Reread today's verses, and decide to believe that whatever your today and your tomorrow bring, that God's strength is more than enough. Begin to memorize one of the verses. If someone has a problem today, tell them about God's mighty promises of strength.

Burying the Past

BEAR WITH EACH OTHER AND FORGIVE WHATEVER
GRIEVANCES YOU MAY HAVE AGAINST ONE ANOTHER.
FORGIVE AS THE LORD FORGAVE YOU.

Colossians 3:13

Sarah put down the phone slowly, *Oh, Lord, I don't believe I still feel this way after all this time!* She'd just found out that in a few days she was going to see her sister-in-law Danielle, whom she hadn't seen or spoken to for fifteen years. Sarah had become a Christian recently—yet the old anger and resentments still rose hot within her.

Although Danielle had once been Sarah's best friend, she had done much to hurt Sarah over a period of years—and never once did Danielle show a bit of remorse. It was only when Danielle moved across the country that Sarah was finally able to get any peace about the relationship.

Sarah knew what she was feeling at this moment wasn't right, for she had memorized the verse, "Be kind and compassionate to one another, forgiving each other, just as in Christ God forgave you" (Ephesians 4:32). Only, now it wasn't just a Bible verse, it was a mirror into her heart. Hand still on the phone, with her heart pounding, Sarah turned to God and asked for His forgiveness.

The next morning during her devotional time she was in Genesis, and *just happened* to be reading the story of Joseph. She read until the last chapter where Joseph's brothers came to ask him for forgiveness for the grievous thing they had done to him. Joseph's godly response in the face of much abuse, and the resulting years of trials, was to let them know God had used for the good what they had meant for evil (Genesis 50:20; Romans 8:28).

Sarah knew God had spoken to her. How could she have thought to withhold what Christ had so freely offered to her? She had forgiven the day before, but God brought her beyond forgiveness to the place where Sarah could see footprints of God in those times.

Sarah realized God used it to mature and strengthen her. And even prepare her for better future relationships.

God then filled Sarah with peace about meeting her sister-in-law. She even began to look forward to seeing Danielle again. Sarah even determined to ask forgiveness of Danielle for her part in the broken relationship.

PRAYER: *Thank You God for Your unconditional for-giveness and grace toward me. Help me Lord, to be quick to forgive others, and slow to remember the hurts. May I have no unforgiveness in my heart toward anyone. For I know that if I don't forgive, then I am sinning against You—and I don't want to do that ever. Help me to remember that love covers a multitude of sins. Amen.*

Make it yours: In your quiet time with the Lord today take time to have the Holy Spirit search your heart if there is any resentment, bitterness, or unforgiveness. Have a pencil and paper to write down if God reveals anything to you. Stay until you are sure that you have forgiven everyone who has ever done you harm. Walk away in the joy and freedom of forgiveness.

No Kingdom Retirement Plan

THEN THE LORD SAID TO HIM,
"WHAT IS THAT IN YOUR HAND?"
Exodus 4:2

Retirees are healthier, more active, and feeling younger than ever before. Many don't retire, they just leave their jobs for something more fulfilling. So it should be for Christians, because God's kingdom doesn't come with a retirement plan this side of heaven.

At fifty-plus, women sometimes have fewer responsibilities and better finances than during younger years. And, they can approach life with experience grown from years of walking with God. While we know every Christian woman is not financially well off, or even wants to be in full-time ministry, the fact is, she is called to serve God—where she is, with the talents God has given her.

Elaine Bohrer, a widow from Sayville, New York, always had a desire to serve God, but didn't know what she could ever do. God caught her attention with a verse and gave her the vision to feed the poor on Long Island: "For I was hungry and you gave me something to eat, I was thirsty and you gave me something to drink, I was a stranger and you invited me in" (Matthew 25:35).

One day, holding a loaf of bread, she thought, *sandwiches I can do.* Armed with ten bologna sandwiches and her faith, she went to feed the hungry.

Fifteen years later, the Lighthouse Mission (which she founded) now feeds and provides guidance and assistance to approximately eighty thousand men, women, and children every year.

Elaine, who thought she had nothing to offer God or people, became a "beacon of light" to bring help to people on Long Island, all because a woman took what she had and used it for God. Elaine didn't believe in retiring.

Moses was another man who didn't think he could serve God, but when He was eighty years old, God called him to lead God's people out of bondage.

You and I may not be called to feed the hungry or to deliver a group of people, but He has called us to use what we have for Him in our world. Like Sister Elaine and Moses, let's not seek to retire from our kingdom job. He calls us not to take it easy, but to come and get a recommissioning. He'll refuel and refire us for the next phase of living.

It is never too late or too early to yield ourselves totally to Him, for His service.

> **PRAYER:** *Oh, Lord, help me be as Moses who by faith left all to follow You. May I hear Your voice and know Your will for my life. Enable me to be willing to follow and serve You, wherever You lead. May I know Your will for my life is always a good one. And may I know You will always be with me. Amen.*

Make it yours: Whatever stage of life you are in, God has work for you to do. He said we are to be about His business until He comes (Ephesians 2:10). Ask Him what you can do for someone today. Then ask if there is something He'd have you do on a regular basis. Write these down and make a plan, no matter how small, and then start to do it. Remember the ten sandwiches.

Searching for Love

I WILL GET UP NOW AND GO ABOUT THE CITY,

THROUGH ITS STREETS AND SQUARES;

I WILL SEARCH FOR THE ONE MY HEART LOVES.

SO I LOOKED FOR HIM BUT DID NOT FIND HIM.

Song of Songs 3:2

Samantha smiled and congratulated her friend on her engagement. Inwardly, Samantha groaned, as once again she was asked to be a bridesmaid. *When is it my turn?* she thought.

Samantha loved God but wanted a husband—soon. She knew life would be perfect if she could just find her prince charming, get married, and start a family.

How many women have thought the same, and after we found prince charming, eventually discovered underneath the shining armor that he's just a man!

The desire to marry is the ultimate goal for many

women around the world. Unfortunately, some women make it the pot of gold at the end of the rainbow. If so, they will continue to be disappointed. For there's no man who can constantly fill the God-shaped hole in our heart for intimacy, passion, and total fulfillment.

God loves us as His one and only. He wants us to seek and love Him, as our one burning desire. He is the Bridegroom, and we're His bride in waiting. Whether we are single, married, childless, widowed, divorced, separated, or anything else in between—we're the focus of His love and passion.

We were created for Him.

But He is not found in the busy streets of our life. We find Him in the inner sanctuary (Psalm 77:13 NKJV). Solomon, the wisest man who ever lived, sought for satisfaction in things. His conclusion: "Meaningless!... Everything is meaningless!" (Ecclesiastes 1:2).

Hannah, in 1 Samuel 1, was stuck in the cultural time when having a child, especially a male child, was the sole value of a woman. Her husband loved her more than his other wife. Yet, she was in anguish and bitterness of soul. His love wasn't enough for her. Elkanah, her husband, would say to her, "Hannah, why are you weeping? Why don't you eat? Why are you downhearted? Don't I mean more to you than ten sons?" (1 Samuel 1:8).

God wants His love to be more than enough for us. Perhaps we're unsatisfied because we're looking for intimacy, confirmation, and satisfaction in something other than God. If we listen with our spirit, will we hear God saying, "Don't I mean more to you than … ?"

PRAYER: *Oh, God, the lover of my soul, how I thank You that You love me even with my sometimes wandering heart. Let me hear You calling me to Your chambers. Help me take my eyes off all that distracts. May I know I was created first and foremost for You. May I know there's only total, complete love, satisfaction, acceptance, intimacy, and passion with You. Every other gift You have given fades in the light of Your lasting love and beauty. Thank You, thank You for loving and waiting for me. I come! Amen.*

Make it yours: Set a time today to meet with your lover. Take your Bible, pen, and paper. Ask Him to reveal what it is that detracts from your dedication and daily walk with Him. Write down what you sense He is speaking to you. Determine to forget what is behind, know you are forgiven, and put Him first today and always. Share with an understanding friend what you have done; encourage her to do the same.

There's a Table Waiting

YOU PREPARE A TABLE BEFORE ME
IN THE PRESENCE OF MY ENEMIES.

Psalm 23:5

The experts tell us that Mother's Day is the biggest eating -out day of the year. It is no wonder why: women for the most part are the ones who daily have the responsibility for food being set on the table, even if it's leftovers or takeout, and then for cleaning up.

I have good news, ladies: we don't have to wait for Mother's Day each year; we don't have to wait for our great wedding feast celebration in heaven either. God has set a table for you here—every day. This may seem too good to be true, but it's true because God said it.

Everything we need for daily victorious living is set on our table (Psalm 23:5). The enemy of our souls wants us to doubt whether God has really given us all we need on our table (that's what tripped up Eve; see Genesis 3). But God has given us everything we need on our table, and it's all found in the Bible (2 Peter 1:3–4).

There's a wonderful story of a missionary's daughter who began to get discouraged when she heard a few instances of God giving special promises to new converts, and she didn't have one. Elizabeth went to her room with her promise box (a little box filled with a Bible verse for each day of the year). She dropped on her knees beside her bed and put it on the bed.

She cried out to God, "Don't you have one for me, just one promise for me?" At this, Elizabeth lifted her hand to reach for the box and accidently hit it, causing all the verses to spill across the floor. Looking at them with tears in her eyes, Elizabeth felt God speak to her heart and say, "Not just one—but all my promises are for you."

"For no matter how many promises God has made, they are 'Yes' in Christ. And so through him the 'Amen' is spoken by us to the glory of God" (2 Corinthians 1:20).

That's what God puts on our table—everything we need for the abundant life. It's better than a king and queen's grand buffet. One day it may be strength we are looking for, as Habakkuk needed when he trembled over what God showed him was coming to Israel. God told Habakkuk that He was strength enough for Habakkuk (Habakkuk 3:16–19).

Maybe by lunchtime some days you are in need of a

good dose of joy. Come to your table and take of the joy of the Spirit. God has set it out for you—don't let it just sit there. As God said to Nehemiah, "This day is sacred to our Lord. Do not grieve, for the joy of the LORD is your strength" (Nehemiah 8:10).

When something comes up that may put fear in your heart or makes you feel alone, tell the enemy you have a table set with the peace of His presence: "Even though I walk through the valley of the shadow of death, I will fear no evil, for you are with me" (Psalm 23:4).

You will never need to worry about your table being bare like Mother Hubbard's cupboard—it's always fully set for you.

Make sure to come and eat before you start your day. If you get hungry later, come and take some more—and always make sure to take enough for those in your world. And then invite them to come for themselves. That's why your cup overflows (Psalm 23:5).

PRAYER: *Dear Lord, thank You for my well stocked table of promises. Hunger me to come and eat daily and then to tell others of Your feast of abundance for them. Amen.*

Make it yours: Read Psalm 23. Pick your favorite verse in it. Meditate on the verse throughout the day and start to memorize it.

He Knows Your Address

WHERE CAN I GO FROM YOUR SPIRIT?
WHERE CAN I FLEE FROM YOUR PRESENCE?

Psalm 139:7

Today you can have joy because there's not a place you can go to get away from God's presence. Others may lose your address or forget where you live—but God never will. He knows where you are every minute of every day.

Whether you're at home, in the store, at work, in the hospital—look around, for God is there with you.

In Genesis 16 is the story of Sarah and her Egyptian slave woman Hagar. Sarah didn't wait for God's timing for His promise of an heir, and she compelled Hagar to bear a child to Abraham instead. When Hagar became pregnant, she flaunted it before her mistress Sarah. In retaliation, Sarah mistreated her—so Hagar ran away.

Hagar was now far from family and friends, completely alone. Trudging through the hot and lonely desert, she surely had fears concerning the outcome for her and her unborn child. Perhaps she thought, *I could die before my baby is born, and no one would even know. How are we to live?*

Just like Hagar faced her impossible situation, we too at times find ourselves in a struggle with no seeming solution. You too may think, is there anyone who cares about me?

Are you a single mom with no help? Are you a frustrated wife with a husband who doesn't seem to understand or care? Are you a wife with no child? Perhaps you never married, or are divorced, or are an abandoned woman, friendless. Despite what personal crisis is yours today, there is someone who cares—Jesus.

God came to Hagar in the desert, and His light permeated the dark night of her soul. God comforted her wounded spirit and gave her direction and the promise of future blessings for her and her unborn son.

Hagar would never forget what God did, for He told her to name her child Ishmael, which means "God Hears." Every time she spoke his name, she'd be reminded of her encounter with the God who cared. She called the place where God met her El Roi, meaning "God who sees us."

Although Hagar lived thousands of years ago, her

story is for us today. Our God is the God of all time and all people.

"Jesus Christ is the same yesterday and today and forever" (Hebrews 13:8).

Just as God worked in Hagar's life, He is working in yours. Sometimes you just have to open your heart to hear His songs of comfort and hope. And if you look in the sand of your desert, you'll see His footprints ahead to lead you out.

> PRAYER: *Thank You Lord that there is not a place I can go but that You are with me. Thank You for all the wonderful promises. Help me be aware of Your presence throughout this day. Open my ears to hear Your voice. Then may I walk close with You, and seek You and Your Word always. Amen.*

Make it yours: Take a few minutes to read the story of Hagar in Genesis 16 and 21. Ask God to open your spiritual eyes to His awesome care for you. Write down what He speaks to you. Share it with someone.

The Power of Joy

Do not grieve,
for the joy of the Lord is your strength.
Nehemiah 8:10

By nature some people are joyful and cheerful no matter what. Then there are the rest of us who have to work at it. Whatever personality type you are, no matter how difficult your day, you can have joy, for you are a child of God.

Norman Cousins found the healing power of laughter and joy when he was diagnosed with a painful disease. He laughed his way to healing by watching hours and hours of funny shows on video. He was healed and wrote a book about the power of joy.[1] Whether he realized it or not, he acted on a scriptural principal: "A cheerful heart is good medicine, but a crushed spirit dries up the bones" (Proverbs 17:22).

When Norman embarked on his healing journey, he was in great pain and surely didn't feel much like laughing, and he also didn't know if it would do any good.

As children of God, we have no doubt as to the outcome. God tells us joy is one of His Holy Spirit perks. Joy is one of the fruits of walking with Him by faith (Galatians 5:22–23).

Habakkuk, a prophet of God, heard a heavy message about what was coming for rebellious Judah. He trembled and shook at the thought of it. However, he was able to say in the face of this coming disaster, "Yet I will rejoice in the LORD, I will be joyful in God my Savior. The Sovereign LORD is my strength; he makes my feet like the feet of a deer, he enables me to go on the heights" (Habakkuk 3:18–19).

We too, in spite of what's on our calendar, whatever bills may be on our desk, whatever the next phone call brings—are never to fear. Perhaps you feel like sitting down and having a pity party. Maybe you want to burn up your to-do lists, or maybe you don't have a full calendar and wish you did. Whatever it is, you can rejoice, for He is your source of joy. He is with you and will never leave you (Nehemiah 8:10; Matthew 28:20).

Yes, days may come when you're weeping inwardly or outwardly over something that seems to have camped on your doorstep. It's then God reminds us, "weeping may

remain for a night, but rejoicing comes in the morning"
(Psalm 30:5).

In the meanwhile, God promises there are special
treasures that only come in the dark places with Him
(Isaiah 45:3). Our times of sorrow are never wasted. We
always come out on the other side—stronger in faith and
closer to God—with joy.

PRAYER: *Dear Lord, thank You for being my source
of joy. Forgive me for the times I forget. Help me to stir
up this joy. Help me not to look around at what I don't
have, or what I do have that I don't want. Help me to
trust You for all I need. Amen.*

Make it yours: Write down one of the verses
above on joy and say it out loud. Keep it with you
today and determine to rejoice, even if you don't feel
like it. Make sure to wake up tomorrow rejoicing in
Him.

Come and Taste and See

TASTE AND SEE THAT THE LORD IS GOOD;
BLESSED IS THE [PERSON] WHO TAKES REFUGE IN HIM.

Psalm 34:8

Women have a reputation for being chocoholics. There's a Pepperidge Farm ad on TV that plays on this—a woman is hiding her Milano chocolate cookies in a ceiling light fixture for future secret consumption.

Yes, in life there are times it seems only chocolate will do. If we're honest, we'll admit it only momentarily satisfies, and that it usually leaves a telltale pound or two to haunt us. Yes, chocolate calls and then disappoints.

Not so with the Lord. He bids us to come—and there's no disappointment. He satisfies totally.

"I am the LORD your God, who brought you up out of Egypt. Open wide your mouth and I will fill it" (Psalm 81:10).

With God you don't have to worry about the taste being bad or adding some pounds. The taste is always good—for He is good.

God's call is a personal invite. You can't send someone else in your place to taste of His good table. No one can taste for you. You have to taste for yourself.

Partake of His goodness today; He's anxiously waiting for you to come! You'll find Him and His goodness in the Word and in the secret place. He wants to walk with you through your day and show you how good good can be. Come into His inner chamber; draw near. You'll see for yourself what the psalmist tells us: "How sweet are your words to my taste, sweeter than honey to my mouth!" (Psalm 119:103).

There are days when you may want to lose heart or get discouraged, and that's the time to let the goodness of the Lord be your rock.

"I am still confident of this: I will see the goodness of the LORD in the land of the living" (Psalm 27:13).

God is so good that He cares about everything. But, I especially love that He even cares about the little things, the unimportant things—but those that are important to me. God has found a beloved lost earring for me; He's fixed my computer, started my car, and even enabled me to tape something on my VCR when it was broken for weeks—just because I asked.

One time, as a new Christian, there was a special

speaker at church who I really wanted to hear, but it was my turn to babysit in the church nursery. I told God (but no one else), that I would babysit because it was my turn to babysit, but I really wanted to hear the speaker. Two days later, God had a dear sister in the Lord tell me she didn't want me to miss this speaker. She said she'd heard him before, and she was going to babysit for me, like it or not. Now, that's a good God!

PRAYER: *Oh, Lord, thank You that I can come and taste and find You are always good. Let my ears daily be open to hear Your call to come. As I go through this day, open my heart to see the good plan You have for me—and may I rejoice in Your goodness. Amen.*

Make it yours: Determine today to look for His goodness. Praise Him as you find this goodness. Before you go to bed, write down one thing that especially blessed you, and go to sleep thanking Him for being so good to you.

Serve with Gladness

SERVE THE LORD WITH GLADNESS.
Psalm 100:2 NKJV

Life won't be tamed no matter how hard we try. There will always be an element of surprise as our days unfold. As Cobham Brewer said, "Man proposes, God disposes."[1] However, with God as our Father, whatever our future holds, it will never be a surprise to God, or a disruption to His purpose for our life. We can therefore serve God—where we are, with what we have—and serve it up with pure gladness.

We can do this not necessarily because of our present circumstances, but, always, because He is in control—always. The plans we have laid out for our life obviously do not include a time of deep financial distress (Philippians 4:19), or period of ill health where we perhaps need to be served, etc. However, even then—we can serve God with joy.

Paul said, "Be joyful always; pray continually; give thanks in all circumstances, for this is God's will for you in Christ Jesus" (1 Thessalonians 5:16–18). Paul knew what he was talking about; tested and tried to the max, he and Silas served God in prison with supersized gladness. They didn't let the prison bars keep them from serving God. They made the gospel and their joy known to all who could hear (Acts 16:22–34).

Barbara served the Lord with gladness in the midst of a deep trial of health. During church worship services at the nursing home, we'd always hear Barbara's voice singing praises above the others—from her stretcher. Afterwards, when we'd try to help her eat the refreshments, she'd say, "Come back after you give others their desserts. I can wait. I am not going anywhere. Meanwhile, be thinking about what I can pray for you guys this month."

Her body may have been imprisoned by a stretcher, but her spirit soared for all to see. Barbara gave more than she took. She served God with gladness where she was.

Perhaps you are now the caretaker of grandchildren or an elderly relative. This can be a thankless, taxing, and seemingly never ending job, making you feel like a prisoner at times. When God calls upon us to serve Him in this way, we can do it with gladness not only because God promises that He will never give us more than we can handle (1 Corinthians 10:13), but because He guarantees we will never go it alone—for He is with us always (Haggai 2:4).

PRAYER: *Dear Lord, thank You that You call me to serve You with gladness wherever, and in whatever circumstances I am. Help me to have joy today. And as I look and wait on You for healing or deliverance from my circumstances (if needed), may I seek opportunities to serve You. For I know there's no small service done for You, and there is no prison that can hold my joy in You. Help me today, not to think of what I don't have, but to shine for You with what I do have. Amen.*

Make it yours: Whatever you are struggling with today (or anticipating in the future), give yourself and it to God. Thank Him for what you do have. If you are in good health, thank Him for it. If not, while you wait for healing, thank Him for the grace in the midst of ill health. Ask Him to open your eyes to the beauty in your life today. Be actively looking for an opportunity to serve by reaching out to someone with what you do have. Put a smile on your face and in your eyes. Determine to serve Him with gladness—no matter what!

Yes, You Can!

I CAN DO EVERYTHING THROUGH HIM WHO GIVES ME
STRENGTH.

Philippians 4:13

A children's classic, *The Little Engine That Could*, is a story about a train engine who attempted something seemingly impossible. He thought he could—and therefore he did.[1]

With the Holy Spirit in us, how much more can we accomplish? And—it won't be because we are so wonderful or confident. It'll be because God is with us; therefore nothing is impossible.

If you're over forty, or you're so far over forty you've stopped counting, you may think you're limited. With God, there are no limits; the best is always around the bend.

Perhaps it's a job interview, another exercise and diet

adventure, driving in a new city, or starting a new business. Whatever it is—you and God together can make it happen. God takes pleasure in challenging people to step out of the box or to take on seemingly insurmountable situations. I believe God chooses to place impossible situations in our paths so we'll have to trust in Him—and He gets the glory.

One night, strong winds fiercely tossed around Peter and the disciples' boat. When Peter saw Jesus walking toward them on the water, his faith rose, and he asked Jesus to tell him to come. Jesus said, "Come," and Peter walked on the water! Peter only sank when he took his eyes off Jesus and looked at the wind.

My son, John, after graduating from the Culinary Institute, dreamed and prayed of going to Italy to apprentice with an Italian chef. At twenty, not knowing a word of Italian, but with faith and family encouragement, he did just that. Upon his returning to New York, his school and soul mate, Russell Cobb, was waiting and felt they should start a frozen dessert business.

With nothing more than hope in God, they started Daystar Desserts in our garage. They outgrew the garage and now have a flourishing business where they make ten thousand cheesecakes a day. And that's not the end of John's impossible dreams. He's waiting on God for a future ministry that'll bring hope and help to those who have lost their way.

You're never too young—or too old.

June Vilandy was in a wheelchair, over one hundred pounds overweight. June said she had so much stress she almost ate herself to death. She was depressed, unable to have necessary surgery because of her weight, and had to rely on oxygen for severe asthma attacks. She indeed had a mountain to climb to become healthy.

Desperate, but with hope, June began a journey of a new way of healthy eating and exercise. It took her a few years, but by staying the course and not giving up, at sixty-two years old, she had regained her health, her joy and good humor, and lost 109 pounds![2]

What is it you think you can't do?

PRAYER: *Oh Lord, help me not look at my age, or my limitations, or how many times I failed, but to You. Open my eyes to what You have for me. May I know with You I can do all things. Amen.*

Make it yours: If there's something you have wanted to do and have perhaps failed at before (perhaps even several times), or haven't yet tried, start today in some small way. Write down your goal and the steps to getting there. Put today's verses across the top of your list. Determine to keep your eyes on Jesus, thereby walking over the water of this seemingly impossible situation.

He Cares for You

CAST ALL YOUR ANXIETY ON HIM
BECAUSE HE CARES FOR YOU.

1 Peter 5:7

Have you ever wondered where the days and the hours go? Does there always seem to be more to do than minutes? The amount of time is the same for all of us. Twenty-four hours in a day, seven days a week, and 365 days a year ... even for Christians.

In our fervor to serve the Lord sometimes we pile too much into too few hours. I know. I've done it way too many times.

At church a few years ago we were holding an outreach to our community. At the beginning of the project I had prayed and committed it to God. However, when the calendar hit fast forward, I clicked into me-mode rather than God-mode.

One day I furiously attempted to finish up the table decorations for this event. The door bell rang, jangling my already uptight nerves. *Oh no,* I moaned, *what does someone want now!*

I couldn't believe I wasn't done with these table centerpieces, still had a doctor's appointment, and needed to shop for dinner. Plus there was a meeting at church that evening—by which time everything was supposed to be finished!

I muttered under my breath and opened the door.

It was my neighbor and friend Sharon. She came in smiling and put down some packages on the counter. "I was making lasagna last night and thought of how you and Frank love it—so I made an extra pan. I brought you salad and fresh Italian bread too."

Sharon then said that she had come to help me finish up the decorations. I couldn't believe it. I had just inwardly complained about the interruption and here it was a gift from God. I'd been overly concerned, and all the while He was taking care of it. Maybe I'd forgotten that I had given it all to Him, but He hadn't.

Sharon put away the food, and I picked up a yet-to-be-finished centerpiece. I instinctively reached to straighten the lopsided Bible verse in the middle of it. The verse couldn't have been more personal if the Lord had emailed it to me from heaven: "Trust in the LORD with all your heart and lean not on your own understanding; in all your ways acknowledge him, and he will make your paths straight" (Proverbs 3:5–6).

The verse spotlighted my lack of trust in Him throughout the past hours. I'd concentrated on things to get done, hours left, and my meager abilities. Had I leaned on Him, I would have rejoiced instead of fretted. However, God is so gracious and merciful. He straightened my bumpy road despite my forgetting that I had cast my cares on Him.

PRAYER: *May I not be so rushed, so pressed in by life that I miss You and all I have to rejoice in. Let me never forget that You care for me, and that my life is in Your hands. May I know I'm not a victim of circumstances and people. Remind me that my days—everything I care about—is in Your loving hands.*

Make it yours: Whatever weighs on you today, or in the weeks to come, write them down and give them to God. Ask for His peace and wisdom. Read today's verse again and say it out loud.

The Power of Encouragement

WE SENT TIMOTHY, WHO IS OUR BROTHER AND
GOD'S FELLOW WORKER IN SPREADING THE GOSPEL OF CHRIST,
TO STRENGTHEN AND ENCOURAGE YOU IN YOUR FAITH.

1 Thessalonians 3:2

It was the eighth time in front of the dressing room mirror with another dress on—and the mirror wasn't cooperating. With each try on, I felt progressively older and heavier, and now a new haircut was in order. At this point, I wasn't sure a free instant liposuction and face lift would even work!

I stared at my reflection and considered either hibernating or coming down with the day-before-the-event flu. Breaking the flow of my schemes, a woman rushed over and said, "I just love that dress. It looks great on you. Can you show me where I can find it?"

One million dollars couldn't have felt better at that

moment. Suddenly, I didn't feel as heavy or as old, and maybe my hair could wait awhile. In fact, keep your cosmetic surgery. I just got encouraged, and the best part was that it didn't cost me anything.

I directed her to find the dress, and danced back to the dressing room, all the while singing, "Glory to God in the Highest." The blessing went on as I encouraged a seemingly harried cashier. I was rewarded with a bright smile.

But, all encouragements are not equal. My momentary pout about what I looked like (which would have passed with the morning light) doesn't compare with someone who perhaps is feeling abandoned and is in dire need of a big thumb's up.

Paul, the great apostle, more than once had been forsaken by people, even his own coworkers. At times he encouraged himself; other times the Lord Himself encouraged him (2 Timothy 4:16–17; Acts 23:11).

In Acts 27, Paul is a prisoner on a ship where fear reigns. Those aboard are in the midst of chaos awaiting sure shipwreck. In the dark of the night, an angel of God appears and encourages Paul. He tells Paul not to be afraid, for God will spare everyone's life. Not only was Paul encouraged, but the next morning he told those aboard the ship that they too could take heart. God was in control, and while the ship would be lost, all lives would be saved.

There will be days it may seem as if our ship will go down. Then God comes to us as He did with Paul, and He tells us not to be afraid (Luke 12:7). He may use His word, a song, or another person. In whatever mode, He will give us encouragement, and our heart will be lighter with the hope of His Word. Then, we can lift our head and go and give that same encouragement to another in need of a hopeful word.

PRAYER: *Lord, how I thank You for Your Word and the Holy Spirit. They whisper hope to me that You are near. I can fear not. Help me, no matter what situations surround today, to know You are with me, and together we can face and deal with anything. Whatever is left over from yesterday, You can handle it too. You love me; You are in control; You will never leave me—therefore all is well. Amen.*

Make it yours: Receive your encouragement from this word today. Be actively looking for an opportunity to pass it along today.

Palace Protocol

ENTER HIS GATES WITH THANKSGIVING AND HIS COURTS
WITH PRAISE; GIVE THANKS TO HIM AND PRAISE HIS NAME.

Psalm 100:4

The infamous Buckingham Palace guards are known for standing ramrod straight, for their bright red tunics and black bearskin hats. You can only get past these guards with proper authorization and identification. Then once inside, there is more protocol to follow. Visiting the home of royalty has strict rules of conduct.

The heavenly palace also has its protocol. It is not surrounded by guards and you don't need a special invite to get in. You just need to be a child of God by faith in Jesus Christ. There is, however, an appointed way to enter His courts.

It doesn't matter what we wear to fellowship with our Lord; we have our white robe of salvation on.

Nonetheless, as we come by faith, we're to come into His gates with thanksgiving, and into His courts with praise (Psalm 100:4).

We can come to Him at the beginning of our day, at the end, or anytime in between. Whenever we come with praise and thanksgiving on our lips, and in our heart, He is blessed, and so are we. Most of the disciplines of the Christian life are for us: prayer, Bible reading, fellowship, etc. But, it is in thanksgiving and praise that the attention is all on God.

Thanksgiving takes our mind off ourselves, our fears, our needs, and puts the focus on Him and His sufficiency. It helps us remember who He is and who we are. We bring to mind the wondrous things about Him and all He does for us always.

Before we even begin our petitions and Bible reading with Him, we have already been blessed. The weights—the cares of life that can bow us over—fall away in the face of thanksgiving and praise.

David was a man who knew the blessing of thanksgiving on both sides. He cried out a lament of pain and distress; yet David said that he would praise God in song and glorify Him with thanksgiving. David knew God would be more pleased with this than if he'd offered an ox or a bull. By coming to God in thanksgiving and praise, David blessed and glorified God, and he came away blessed and free (Psalm 69:29–36).

There will be times we come barging into the throne room without praise and thanksgiving for an immediate need or worry, but He bids us welcome anyway. For when we make praise and thanksgiving a beloved part of our devotions, they are in our heart and will rise again.

PRAYER: *Thank You Lord, that You haven't left us clueless as to Your desires when we come into Your heavenly throne. Help me to enter with a heart and a mouth full of thanksgiving and praise for all You are and all You do. Thank You, thank You, and thank You. Amen.*

Make it yours: During your time with God today, set aside a few minutes before reading the Word or prayer to just think on Him. Let the thanksgiving and praise flow from you to Him. If you are in the habit of doing this—increase it by a few minutes today. Read a psalm out loud in praise to Him.

Me, Lord?

THE LORD SAID TO HIM, "WHO GAVE MAN HIS MOUTH?
WHO MAKES HIM DEAF OR MUTE? WHO GIVES HIM SIGHT OR
MAKES HIM BLIND? IS IT NOT I, THE LORD? NOW GO;
I WILL HELP YOU SPEAK AND WILL TEACH YOU WHAT TO SAY."
Exodus 4:11 – 12

The church and the Bible are filled with examples of men and women who just knew they couldn't be used by God.

Moses was called to lead God's people out of Egypt. Jeremiah was ordained as a prophet to a stiff-necked generation. The common denominator was their resistance to the call. They both feared for differing reasons (Exodus 3; Jeremiah 1).

Every child of God has a call. You are not Moses, and you're not Jeremiah. But, you are you, and God says you are ordained to be His disciple in your world. You have been given gifts and talents, and your world is waiting to be blessed by them, in a way only you can do.

Moses used the excuse that he wasn't eloquent; he didn't think he could speak well at all. I can identify with that. I failed speech class in high school. God must have roared that day knowing years later I would be in the ministry. God knew what He was doing—for it has been good for me. Knowing I don't have a natural gift for speaking makes me rely on God, and not myself.

Jeremiah used the excuse that he was a mere child. God's answer was, "Do not say, 'I am a youth' … you shall go … you shall speak … do not be afraid … for I am with you" (Jeremiah 1:7–8 NKJV).

There is never anyone God calls that He doesn't promise that He will be with, even as He did with Jeremiah, Moses, and Joshua (Joshua 1).

Yes, Jeremiah was young, as was David who later became the king. So was a ten-year-old boy, Zach Bonner, of Valarico, Florida. He used what God had given him and walked 280 miles and raised $25,000 for homeless children. He was faithful, and even walked on Thanksgiving and his birthday.[1]

On the chance you may think you are too old—think again. Moses was eighty and went strong for forty more years.

Have you ever been asked to do something you didn't think you could do? Perhaps you were asked to teach

Sunday school or to lead a Bible class. Maybe you were asked to give a testimony. Your first thought may have been, *Me, Lord?*

After the first thought of *why you*, remember God has called you, He has equipped you, and best of all, He will be with you. How can you say *no* to Him who said *yes* to the cross for you?

PRAYER: *Lord, thank You that You have given me gifts and talents, even if I don't feel like You have. Forgive me for the times I have said no. Commission me again. Open my eyes as to how I can be used today. Help me know there are no small jobs for You. And that You will always be with me. Amen.*

Make it yours: Wait upon God, and write a list of what you think He'd have you do for Him today, or what He might be calling you to do as an ongoing ministry. Tell Him, "Me, Lord!" and then be still and listen.

Heavenly Bank Account

AND MY GOD WILL MEET ALL YOUR NEEDS ACCORDING
TO HIS GLORIOUS RICHES IN CHRIST JESUS.

Philippians 4:19

There is an inscription on the General Post Office building of New York City: "Neither snow nor rain nor heat nor gloom of night stays these couriers from the swift completion of their appointed rounds."

Days come when we want the mail person to forget all about that motto, pass our mailbox with our bills in hand, and deliver them to the rich man on the next block. Unfortunately, that doesn't happen.

On these days we don't want to face what is in the mail, or on the answering machine. Kids in college, medical bills, unforeseen emergencies, unemployment, broken down cars, etc.—we have to deal with them.

At times we are taken by surprise, but God never is;

and there is never a lack in His economy. It may take patience and stretching of our faith (Hebrews 6:12), but He promises He will provide. And occasionally He has some ingenious ways of doing it. In the book of Matthew, when Jesus and Peter had no money for the required taxes, Jesus told Peter, "But so that we may not offend them, go to the lake and throw out your line. Take the first fish you catch; open its mouth and you will find a four-drachma coin. Take it and give it to them for my tax and yours" (Matthew 17:27).

Peter didn't have to worry about his lack of money, for God was with Him. God is with us today too, and we have all His promises to provide for us—even if we've made a mistake. Any mistake we've made is covered by His grace and mercy, which are new every day.

In the days of Elisha, a widow of a prophet had creditors who were going to enslave her two sons to satisfy the bills owed. She had no resources—just a little oil. God sends Elisha, and with him came a miracle for this desperate widow. In her case, it was through the supernatural increase of oil, which put her in a thriving oil business (2 Kings 4:1–7).

Elisha asked the widow, "Tell me, what do you have in your house?" She gave it to God, and He increased it (verse 2). Just a little oil, and God makes a miracle!

Maybe you have nothing to give God except your request and faith. That's enough. He says to come, to ask, and then to expect Him to answer. He will answer. He is a good Father; He delights in providing for His children.

If you don't have any financial worries, thank the Lord. But, trials come to us all in various sizes and shapes, and you too can bank on His promises.

> **PRAYER:** *Thank You Father that You have promised to meet all of our needs. Thank You there is not one promise that has failed in Your Word. And thank You for Your promise to meet them, not according to my meager means, but according to Your riches in glory—which are inexhaustible. May I wait in faith and patience! Amen.*

Make it yours: Write down every need you have. Across the top of the page, write out Philippians 4:19. In the place of "your" in the verse—put your name. Read it out loud, and remind yourself when the fears and doubts come again.

So, You Think No One Understands You?

Women can be complex and hard to understand at times. For years men have tried to figure us out. The fact is—no one will ever totally understand the female species, especially men. We don't even understand ourselves at times; how can we expect a male to understand?

In Genesis 21:8–21, we find Hagar again in a place of desperation. No one knew where she was, or understood what she was going through—or even seemed to care. But, God knew where she was and God cared.

This was not the first time God came to Hagar in a black night of her life, with no seeming hope of a sunrise. Hagar was in the desert again. Perhaps she thought, *What did I do to deserve this? I served my master Abraham and mistress Sarah faithfully—and they throw me and my son out with nothing but a piece of bread and a skin of water!*

Hagar herself probably didn't understand her own raging questions and fears. Eventually, Hagar resigned herself to the inevitable death of her son from thirst. She sat down and wept in despair, for she had forgotten the one who had come to her aid years before. But—God didn't forget Hagar: "God called to Hagar from heaven and said to her, 'What is the matter, Hagar? Do not be afraid; God has heard the boy crying as he lies there'" (Genesis 21:17).

God was saying, "Have you forgotten what I promised last time—that I have a good plan for you and your son's future? There's nothing to fear." He opened her eyes to a well of water nearby, and Hagar knew once again that there was one who understood her heartache!

People in our lives sometimes mean well, but just don't or can't always understand how we feel. There are times we don't have someone in our life, as Hagar didn't, with whom we're intimate enough to even try to share how we feel.

Maybe today you're in a quandary you don't understand yourself. You don't know how you got there, or even what to think about it. Like Hagar, you've forgotten the promises of God, and are crying out in distress.

As a daughter of God, you never need to cry in despair; instead cry out with hope to Him.

He will hear, and He will remind you too of His precious, all sufficient love and care. Open your eyes. Look around and you'll see, as Hagar, the well of water God has provided in your desert place.

> **PRAYER:** *Dear Lord, thank You for Your Word and all its promises to me. Help me to know even when I don't understand myself, that You understand. Set me free from having to understand everything. You don't tell me I have to understand; You tell me to believe and trust You. May I be as a child who just trusts in the love and watchful care of her Father. Amen.*

Make it yours: Whatever things you are having trouble understanding, or figuring out, write them down and give them to God—and forget about them. Trust Him that if He wants you to understand, you will. And if not, you will trust Him anyway.

Hold the Sunrise!

> BE STRONG AND TAKE HEART,
> ALL YOU WHO HOPE IN THE LORD.
>
> *Psalm 31:24*

In God's economy each day is another beginning—a hope to get us out of bed. Nonetheless, life sometimes throws us a day when we want to say, "Hold that sunrise."

I had one of those recently. For the past weeks I'd been faced with back to back disappointments, reversals, and hurts in the ministry (it comes with the territory). Usually, I bounce back quickly—but not this time. For three nights I went to bed weary and woke up weary. The gray sky seemed as dim as my attitude this morning. I lay in bed and complained to God, "I am getting too old for this." And just on the chance He didn't hear me, I repeated it, "Plain and simple—I'm getting too old!"

Continuing on this road of self-pity, the thought

floated by that if I can't take it, maybe it's time to step down from ministry. At that moment it sounded good to me.

With this cheery mindset, I wasn't ready to face the day yet. I rolled over and picked up my book on the night table. My eyes were drawn to the verse on the bookmark:

> The righteous will flourish like a palm tree, they will grow like a cedar of Lebanon; planted in the house of the LORD, they will flourish in the courts of our God. They will still bear fruit in old age, they will stay fresh and green, proclaiming, "The LORD is upright; he is my Rock, and there is no wickedness in him."
>
> PSALM 92:12–15

I had held this bookmark many times, but this morning it was a special delivery telegram just for me! Yes, I was way over-the-hill age wise—but, God's strength didn't leave me on the top of the hill.

He let me know loud and clear that He was my strength. He would make sure I would still bear fruit even in old age because I am planted in His court.

The circumstances had not changed in those few minutes, but my thinking had. I was reminded that whether I was thirty or one hundred, it wasn't me who had to have the strength and joy to face the challenges of my life.

Even Sarah never would have thought she'd have strength to bear a child when her childbearing clock had stopped ticking. Nonetheless, Sarah had strength enough—for God gave it to her (Hebrews 11:11).

It wasn't Sarah, and it isn't me or you who have to worry about bearing fruit for God. He'll make sure we have His stamina for the journey, and He'll bring forth the fruit. Once again, I had to trust not myself, but Him. That I can do!

PRAYER: *Lord, thank You that when I am discouraged, and when I want to sit out the day, I can always come to You for a refilling of my strength. In myself I'm weak. It is only in You, I can accomplish what You have put on my plate today. It is only in You, I can bear fruit at any age. It is only in You, I can be fresh and flourishing. Remind me always from whence comes my help. Amen.*

Make it yours: Whatever God has given you to do, and you think you can't do, give it to Him. By faith in Him, believe and know that you and God together can accomplish it.

Are You Hungry?

THEN JESUS DECLARED, "I AM THE BREAD OF LIFE.
HE WHO COMES TO ME WILL NEVER GO HUNGRY,
AND HE WHO BELIEVES IN ME WILL NEVER BE THIRSTY."

John 6:35

"Are you hunnng-reeey?" a jovial woman cries advertising cereal on TV. She's so convincingly happy, you want to run and taste her cereal—just on the chance it'll make you smile too. The cereal may be good, but it will only satisfy for the moment, and, soon enough you'll be hungry again.

God says people don't live by bread alone. Food will feed our body, but never our soul. It is God and His Word alone that will satisfy our spirit (Deuteronomy 8:3).

Esau, Isaac's son, found this out the hard way. He was so physically hungry that he gave away his spiritual blessing for a pot of lentils (Genesis 25:19–34). Afterward, though he wept bitterly, he was unable to get it back (Hebrews 12:16–17).

Religious disciplines won't feed us either; it's God our hearts long for. Most women know that when we want chocolate, only chocolate will do. And, when our spirits are dry, it's only by fellowshipping with Him that we will be satiated. Jacob, who loved Rachel, willingly worked seven years so that she could be his wife; then on the eve of his wedding, he was tricked and given Leah instead. In order to truly have Rachel, Jacob had to agree to another seven years of labor, which he did. Then, and only then, was Jacob satisfied—with Rachel's, not Leah's, arms around him.

King David could have all his heart desired, yet his hunger and thirst were only fulfilled in the inner sanctuary where God's presence was:

> O God, you are my God, earnestly I seek you; my soul thirsts for you, my body longs for you, in a dry and weary land where there is no water. I have seen you in the sanctuary and beheld your power and your glory.
>
> PSALM 63:1–2

God calls us to guard our hearts and be like David, for sometimes we can carry our "doing" mentality into our Christian life. We can get so busy working for the Lord, that at times we may substitute works for an intimate love relationship with Him. It's then we will find ourselves discontent, because we have fed and drank of God's work, and not of Him.

Today, before you hit the runway, come to Him to fill your soul. If not, each step you take will drain you, and by midday you'll begin to be dry and hungry for God. When you come to His well in the morning to drink, He makes sure you have more than enough. Like a camel that stores water for the dry, hot desert, when life quenches you, you'll automatically switch to your reserve tank.

PRAYER: *Oh, Lord, thank You for spiritual hunger and thirst, for without it, we wouldn't seek You, and we'd become weak and ineffectual for You and Your kingdom. May I heed Your call daily to come to the well—the source of all life—You. Praise You that You fill my soul with true life and satisfaction. Keep calling and wooing me. I come. Amen.*

Make it yours: Read Psalm 63:1–4 again. When you become hungry today or sit down to eat, make a point of thinking of the Lord and how you want to hunger more for Him. Then pick up the Word, and feast on heavenly food—even if only for a few minutes.

Walk Free

THEREFORE, SINCE WE ARE SURROUNDED
BY SUCH A GREAT CLOUD OF WITNESSES, LET US THROW OFF
EVERYTHING THAT HINDERS AND THE SIN THAT SO EASILY
ENTANGLES, AND LET US RUN WITH PERSEVERANCE THE RACE
MARKED OUT FOR US. LET US FIX OUR EYES ON JESUS,
THE AUTHOR AND PERFECTER OF OUR FAITH.

Hebrews 12:1 – 2

Put on your running shoes—you're in a race! It's not a race measured by the clock, and it's not the daily race we sometimes run with overflowing schedule and commitments.

It's the race of all races—the one we started the day of our salvation. It's a race to be enjoyed, and one with our own personal trainer alongside.

While God calls us to run our best, He doesn't want us to carry fears or worries while running His course. He wants us to run with Him, full of joy, free of entanglements.

He hasn't left us clueless—we have His Word, which reveals the obstacles and is filled with the good news on how to run light. Jesus not only set us free from the penalty of our sins—but He also died to set us free from its power (Romans 6–8). What does that mean to us? It means we don't have to be captive to anything or anyone that would have an ungodly hold on us.

There is an ad where a woman is walking down the street with a chain around her ankle, dragging a scale. With this I can identify. Every morning for years, the first thing I did was get on the scale; how my day began was determined by the number. Over time, God revealed my problem wasn't the scale, or the food—it was my being consumed with them.

However, when I looked to Jesus and not myself, He showed me that He came not only to save me from my sins but "to proclaim freedom for the captives [me and you] and release from darkness for the prisoners" (Isaiah 61:1).

I realized I had been set free from the tyranny of the scale. Then by faith in Him and His Word I began to walk it out. (I am still working on the eating part.)

Not everyone has a problem with food or their weight. But, everyone has sin which can trip them up if they are not vigilant. Perhaps they're dragging people around on a chain—children, spouses, parents, bosses, neighbors, or family. How their day goes and where they move depend not so much on God and His leading, but on how these people factor in.

Then there are the weights in life of finances, pregnancy, other people's opinions, and many other trappings. Whatever it is that consumes our thinking, guides our decisions, brings us unrest continually, and leads away from God's guidance is an entanglement. Paul tells us we're to run light, with purpose. He had to make his mind and body his slave that he might win, and not be disqualified for the reward. May we follow Paul's example in our race (1 Corinthians 9:24–27).

> PRAYER: *Lord, how I thank You I am set free from the power of sin. Help me to walk in the light of Your blood-bought freedom. Reveal to me the weights and entanglements which slow me down in my race for, and with, You. I want to run free and with joy. Amen.*

Make it yours: In your quiet time, pray the above prayer. With pen, paper, and the Word, wait on Him, and whatever He reveals to you, repent of it, then give it to Him and run free.

Living to the Max

I HAVE COME THAT THEY MAY HAVE LIFE,
AND HAVE IT TO THE FULL.

John 10:10

Breathing is no guarantee of a life being lived to the fullest. Living to the max is a determined, planned, disciplined life—it doesn't happen by accident.

Jesus came and lived His life to the fullness for which He was created. He was born with a purpose. Everything He did was with that end goal in sight (Luke 9:51).

His destiny was to complete the Father's work of redemption at Calvary. Meanwhile, He was the living embodiment of the Father's love.

Each morning we arise, we have a destiny to fulfill. In our world we are the living representative of the great love of God. In our unique way, we can be walking out His glorious plan for our life—and be used to affect those around us for good.

Whatever He has before us—it's an opportunity to live the abundant life.

God doesn't ask us to do it in our strength. Jesus sent the Holy Spirit to empower us to live a life overflowing with His abundance.

The plan God has laid out for us is like a railroad track. We are the train, and the Holy Spirit is the power to run the train. Jesus is the engineer, and the Father is back in the control tower, in charge of it all.

When we stay on track and draw on His power, and follow the directions from the engineer and the Father—we're living life to the max and advancing in the kingdom.

If we decide we don't want to follow the directions from on high, and we jump off the tracks, we cut ourselves off from our power source. And we will not be living life to the max for which we were created. The Bible is filled with saints who set their face to ride the kingdom tracks. When they slip, slow down, or jump the track, they get right back on.

David had a heart for God, but when he sinned with Bathsheba, he derailed. When confronted, David repented and got right back on track to the abundant life (Psalm 51).

It's not always sin that causes us to lose the abundant life; not heeding the whistle to change tracks can cause us to miss it.

Tina and Greg Kemper from Long Island, and their two children, were right on track living the normal Christian life. Tina worked with women's ministry, and Greg was a part-time youth pastor in their local church; the kids were involved—life was good.

One day, God surprised them with a call to the pastorate. After seeking the Lord, Tina and Greg listened to the control tower and switched tracks. They ventured into the unknown—to live on the edge with God to pastor Point Lookout Community Church; God used them to awaken a comatose church into a vibrant, growing church.

If they hadn't taken God's challenge, they would've forfeited the abundant life—and settled for the ordinary.

We're called to the max life—every day. Walking with Him daily and listening for His leading on which track to take, we too will live to the utmost.

PRAYER: *Lord, thank You for the call to live life to the fullest. Help me listen for Your voice—then may I follow. Amen.*

Make it yours: Prayerfully consider what living life to the max is for you—daily and long-range. Write it down and with His help, start walking it out.

Down Home Family Living

CONSEQUENTLY, YOU ARE NO LONGER FOREIGNERS
AND ALIENS, BUT FELLOW CITIZENS WITH GOD'S PEOPLE
AND MEMBERS OF GOD'S HOUSEHOLD.

Ephesians 2:19

Whatever your circumstances, when you belong to God you have a family, and wherever you congregate is God's house.

Every family has conflicts sometimes, yet they love and take care of one another. It's no different in God's family—only more so. God says they'll know we're Christians by our love for one another (John 13:35).

Prince of Peace Church in Long Island may be small in numbers, but the people are big on reaching out to one another. Josephine has cancer and must go for chemo treatments several times a month. Angela drives and coordinates with other church members like Carolyn, who feels bad when she can't drive, and Mariaelena, who drives even when she'll be late for work. At this house, family comes first.

Another member, Sue, has medication problems, making her unable to drive. The church rallied in prayer and became its own answer. Two or three times a week, Frank and Steve get Sue back and forth to church and Bible study. Angela again came alongside; she also drives Sue, and brings her to doctors, monitors her medication, then calls her twice a day to check Sue's drug-taking.

We're seeing a family love-miracle in our house.

You can't go anywhere to get away from your spiritual family either. Wherever you go — you have a relative in town.

My husband and I were in upstate New York at our vacation home when the crippling flood of June 2006 hit us. Thank God, our house was fine. We had water and full cabinets, but no electricity; only intermittent phone; and the two bridges on our road were down — making us stranded for days.

We were two hundred miles from our house and family in Long Island, but we had Christian family in town. Sitting enjoying the beauty and quiet, we saw coming up the hill our brother and sister in the Lord, Larry and Celia McCallin, and they were carrying a big bag of ice. They had driven six miles by car, borrowed an ATV (the only way to travel for several miles), climbed down a ladder on one side of the bridge, up the other—all to bring us ice. Now that's God's family in action!

What about at your house? What are you doing to help carry someone's burden (Galatians 6:2)?

Our Father gave the love call to help everyone we can, especially our church family (Galatians 6:10). He says to pray, to strengthen, to give, and to come alongside. You can never outdo God, and as you help someone, He'll meet your need. Together we make it happen (Ephesians 4:16).

Today, as you go through your day, remember you have a family; you have a second home (God's house), plus a great retirement home waiting.

PRAYER: *Thank You Father that You have adopted me into Your wonderful family, and I have a forever home. Help me to love, to pray, and to reach out to build a true household of God, Amen.*

Make it yours: Make a list of the needs you are aware of in your church/neighborhood. Pray for each one, and ask God if there's something you can do to help with any of the needs. Step out in faith and do it.

Extreme Makeover

> DO NOT CONFORM ANY LONGER TO THE
> PATTERN OF THIS WORLD, BUT BE TRANSFORMED
> BY THE RENEWING OF YOUR MIND.
>
> *Romans 12:2*

Extreme makeover shows seem to be a staple on TV. One features an extreme makeover for women. In one hour, an ordinary woman goes from frump to fabulous.

Most of us would love a personal makeover—however, a woman of God doesn't want only to look good outwardly—she wants to look lovely inside.

Sometimes as we age it's harder to face an ungodly settled-in habit and begin the eviction process. But it can be done if we commit. The new woman in the makeover show didn't just happen. It took time, money, and a crew of professionals. We too need to commit to a journey of inward transformation.

God tells us no matter how long and how comfortable we are with a habit, if it's not good and doesn't honor our Father, it goes. If not, it can have disastrous results down the line, as happened with King Saul.

King Saul was consumed with jealousy toward David. Relentlessly, he hunted down David to destroy him. Saul's anger was such a part of him, he couldn't see it. When Saul's son Jonathon tried to reason with him for the second time concerning his unjust treatment of David, not only did Saul not listen, he tried to kill Jonathon (1 Samuel 20:32–33).

Unfortunately, we have all known similar people. They won't listen, they won't change, and as a result, perhaps have lost jobs, friends, or even spouses.

I had a friend whose parents divorced after thirty years because the husband refused to change his complaining, negative ways. He declared he was too old to change; he was what he was. He loved his wife, but refused to change. He's now a bitter, old, lonely man—all because he wouldn't try to change.

But, as children of God, we are called to change. Just as we need a mirror to see how we're progressing in our makeover, we need the mirror of His Word to reflect the image we're striving for, and to evaluate how we are doing.

In this journey of renewal, we are not alone. God has given us the Holy Spirit to come alongside and help in our lifelong makeover to be like Him. It is by yielding to His gentle leading we become God's sweet aroma in our world, and a showcase for His fruits, such as love, joy, peace, etc. (Galatians 5:22–23).

As a daughter of God, through our lifelong ongoing makeover, we clothe ourselves with the heavenly scent of Jesus Himself: "Rather, clothe yourselves with the Lord Jesus Christ, and do not think about how to gratify the desires of the sinful nature" (Romans 13:14).

Walk tall and beautiful, giving off the tantalizing fragrance of your heavenly Father today. Show people they too can change by the power of Christ. Salt them for Him; He'll be walking by your side smiling and whispering, "Well done, my beloved, sweet smelling daughter."

PRAYER: *Father, help me be like You. Show me what I have to change today to reflect Your image to the people in my life. Amen.*

Make it yours: Read Colossians 3:8–15. Ask God to show you what to next start working on to further your Christian beauty makeover. And make sure to clothe yourself with the Lord today (Romans 13:14).

Red Hot Prayers

THE PRAYER OF A RIGHTEOUS [PERSON]
IS POWERFUL AND EFFECTIVE.

James 5:16

Kids know how to ask—and they know how to ask with passion—when they really want something. Yet, if they ask once and don't seem to care enough to ask again, we get the feeling it's not that important to them.

However, if your daughter comes and throws herself on the floor, grabs your feet, and groans that she absolutely will die if she doesn't get such and such—and then offers to do dishes for a month and throws in a massage—you know she really wants it.

I believe it's not much different with God. Sometimes He'd like to see a little desire and passion when we come with our list. John Knox, the Protestant Reformer, was such a man. His beloved Scotland was without the gospel and soaked in superstition. In the midst of this, John Knox was known for his preaching and passionate prayers.

One time, John knelt to pray in the garden of his church and was overheard crying out in agony of spirit, "Great God, give me Scotland, or I die." This godly man's prayers of passion began the transformation of Scotland. He died with Scotland a paragon of Christianity.[1]

Hannah was childless; she too ran to God in anguish and bitterness of soul. She passionately poured her heart before Him. Hannah so desired a male child, she promised to give him back to the Lord. God heard the passionate cry of Hannah and answered. She became the mother of Samuel the prophet (1 Samuel 1).

Through the years I have prayed many prayers, and God graciously has answered many (I'm still waiting for some). I've prayed at times as if I had a shopping list, and at others times I have prayed with great zeal and desire.

One prayer very heavy on my heart was a double header. Having been disappointed several times, my son John and his wife Holly were going again to the doctor to see if she was pregnant. The same day, my daughter, Maria Elena, and I were going to the doctor with my grandson J. C. to see if he needed more surgery (he had already been through several).

I cried out, "Oh Lord, please, don't let it be one without the other." I wanted both!

God was faithful, and the family was able to celebrate

God's goodness to us. Not only was Holly pregnant—it was twins. Not only did J. C. not need surgery—the doctor was so impressed with his recovery, he wanted to use J. C. as a case study.

My passion—our passion—moved the heart of God. God not only looks for prayers with passion—He wants to hear some BIG prayers. Prayers that only He could answer. A plaque I have expresses it well:

God answers all prayers.
Sometimes He says Yes.
Sometimes He says No, and
Sometimes He says …
You've got to be kidding!!!

I have a feeling when Elijah prayed for no rain, God said, "You got to be kidding me, Elijah!" However, the earnestness of Elijah brought the answer from heaven; it didn't rain for three and a half years—all because one man prayed (James 5:17–18).

PRAYER: *Oh, Lord, teach me to pray BIG prayers that delight You with their passion. Amen.*

Make it yours: Go over your prayer list. Pick one that's dear to your heart. Find a verse that covers it and pray it with passion, reminding God of what He has promised in His Word.

Delighting in His Word

YOUR STATUTES ARE MY DELIGHT;

THEY ARE MY COUNSELORS.

Psalm 119:24

The experts who make the various lists of bestselling books agree that the Bible, by far, is the bestselling book of all time (four to six billion copies sold).[1]

Why has the Bible withstood the test of time and attempts at annihilation? Because it is God's living Word.

With His Word He has given the Holy Spirit to reveal the depths of love, wisdom, and knowledge within its pages. It overflows with everything needed for life and godliness (2 Peter 1:3). And it's in His Word that we meet with God.

Nothing worthwhile ever just happens. It takes planning and preparation. Just as with our daily eating, the food has to be bought and cooked, and the table set, so it is with partaking of the Word. If we don't take the time and effort, it will stay undone, and eventually we'll become spiritually anemic.

We should never think of reading our Bible as just another chore to check off. Open His Word and hear God's sweet voice saying, "Delight in me as I do you. Tarry with me at my table, eat till full, and then leave with an overflow for others."

It's worth whatever it takes to make it happen.

One time, my husband and I were going to visit a couple we hadn't seen in awhile. I was ready early and a little apprehensive, and I wanted to spend time with the Lord about it.

I looked at my chair where I usually sit to read and pray; it was covered with clothes and stuff. The table with my Bible was overflowing and had to be cleaned off. I sighed, and thought, *it isn't worth the effort for such a short time*.

Immediately, the Lord spoke to my heart, *If you were going to spend time with Frank (my husband), wouldn't you expectantly prepare yourself and the bedroom?* Quicker than quick, I dumped the clothes on the bed, grabbed my Bible, and fell in the chair.

What I would have missed! It has become one of my treasured God moments—better than wine and perfume (Song of Songs 1:2–3).

Not only is His Word your sweetest love song, it's all the wisdom and guidance you need. It's the light to guide you through the pathways of life. It's joy when there seems to be nothing to rejoice about. And when you're the weakest, it will carry you (Psalms 32:8; 119:105; 28:7; 94:19).

For thirty-seven years, the evergreen Word of God has been my love and my delight—not one Word has *ever* failed me! It's never lost its power to sustain and strengthen. It has only grown sweeter as the years go by. It will for you too.

Now—go prepare your place, sit down, and eat. Enjoy!

PRAYER: *Lord, thank You for the Word which has brought me You. Help me to love it and You more and more. May I put my walk with You above all else. Help me today to make a deliberate decision to spend time daily at Your feet. May I know there is nothing more important, nothing more joyful than You and Your Word. Amen.*

Make it yours: Read Proverbs 8:34. Think and pray about how much time you'd like to spend with the Lord and His Word daily. Write it down and ask God to help you do it.

Dancing with the Star

LET THEM PRAISE HIS NAME WITH DANCING
AND MAKE MUSIC TO HIM WITH TAMBOURINE AND HARP.
FOR THE LORD TAKES DELIGHT IN HIS PEOPLE.

Psalm 149:3 – 4

One of the reasons *Dancing with the Stars* is a popular TV show is that many people love dancing, even if is just to watch.

Maybe there'll be dancing in heaven at our wedding feast (Revelation 19:7). I think so—because God loves dancing. And He delights in us celebrating His great deeds with passion and love.

Don't worry if you aren't a professional dancer, or if you think you're not a good dancer—you won't even have to take lessons. God wants you to come and rejoice over Him—even as He rejoices over you (Zephaniah 3:17).

It's a worldwide custom to mark life's joyous events, and to acknowledge someone who's made a contribution to society by a celebration in their honor. How much more can we celebrate our salvation, God, and what He has done for us than to come and bring Him joy by acknowledging and commemorating His goodness with happy, uninhibited worship?

Not everyone is demonstrative in their praise. However, we all can show enthusiasm and passion in our worship. We can start by trying it alone; God will be blessed, and we will too.

When I go upstate to Hancock, New York, there's a precious fellowship of sisters-in-the Lord who express their adoration and worship with beautiful flowing yardage of multicolored materials. They form a circle, or two lines, each holding an end of the material. They wave them gracefully up and down with coordinated, yet spontaneous song and dance in harmony while a sister softly plays a psaltry or a Celtic harp.

It's divine celebration with the beauty of heartfelt unabashed praise. Mostly, I've enjoyed watching. But, I'm working up to participating, for I feel the Lord's smile and sense the angels joining in. I think I hear His hands clapping as He enjoys His show of adoration.

Let's be like Miriam, who after God delivered the people by parting the Red Sea, sang and played tambourines and danced with joy in exaltation (Exodus 15:20).

David danced before the Lord with all his might when the ark of the Lord was brought back. His wife, Michal, mocked him, and David responded by saying that he did it for the Lord; and if he were humiliated, he'd do it anyway, and more, for what God had done for him (2 Samuel 6:13–23).

Let's be like children, who with the slightest provocation, dance around for joy without a thought of embarrassment. After all, we are the King's kids, and He loves for us to enjoy ourselves before Him.

Listen, and you'll hear Him whisper, "Put my name first (in permanent ink) on your dance card. The first dance always belongs to me." When we come into His heavenly ballroom, let's not think we're dancing with merely a celebrity or star. We're dancing with The Star!

PRAYER: *Oh Lord, thank You for calling me to celebrate You and Your greatness. Help me to come unashamedly with joy into Your presence. Help me come like David and freely worship You as You desire. Amen.*

Make it yours: Start your devotions by reading Psalm 149. Worship God today in an out-of-the-ordinary way. God will love it, and so will you.

Vanilla, or Chocolate?

We old timers (anyone over 13) can learn from listening to children pray. They have no problem asking for what they want or even letting God know when they want it. In our youth discipleship program, *The Lord's Army*, one of my favorite parts was hearing the kids pray. Now that they've grown (meaning they're teenagers), we'd settle to hear any uncoerced prayer from their lips.

Inevitably, they'd all ask to have a nice day. If it was winter, they'd pray for snow. And when they did—it snowed. (Obviously they didn't pray every week for snow.) They knew just the right time to pray. One time, they had faith to pray it would snow enough to close the school. We, of course, attempted to set them straight about that one—but the next day school closed due to snow!

At one meeting, one of these faith-warriors had the audacity to pray there'd be chocolate ice cream at snack time after the meeting. Guess what, one of the moms came in later, not only with chocolate but vanilla too—therefore everyone was happy.

Oh, we of little faith! When was the last time we asked God to give us a nice day, or for snow just to play in, or for chocolate ice cream?

These soldiers also prayed for missionaries, the president, and the needs of the church with the same simple faith. They were such prayer warriors that people in church had a special box to put their requests in so the Lord's Army would pray. And pray they did—and they saw answers.

These kids were too young to be hindered by religion. They all had grown up in the church hearing God not only saved them, but He loved them and even wanted them to have a good day, and they really believed it when God said,

> Ask and it will be given to you; seek and you will find; knock and the door will be opened to you. For everyone who asks receives; he who seeks finds; and to him who knocks, the door will be opened. If you, then, though you are evil, know how to give good gifts to your children, how much more will

your Father in heaven give good gifts to those who ask him!

MATTHEW 7:7–8, 11

Jabez was a man who had the faith of a child. He prayed not only for God to bless him, but that God would increase his territory—what nerve! God didn't think so: He gave Jabez what he asked for (1 Chronicles 4:10).

Today, God has an inexhaustible well of abundance for you. He bids you to come sit down and enjoy Him. Then take the prayer bucket He has given you, let it down, and draw up His sweet promises. Enjoy, fill your reservoir to overflowing, and go tell others of His goodness waiting for them too.

PRAYER: *Oh Lord, give me the faith of a child to believe all Your promises are for me too. May I delight in You and know that as I do, You will give me the desires of my heart. Amen.*

Make it yours: Today delight in Him, make a list of your desires, give them to Him, and start praying—and keep praying—and be looking for the answer.

Hospital for Broken Hearts

HE HAS SENT ME TO BIND UP

THE BROKENHEARTED, TO PROCLAIM FREEDOM

FOR THE CAPTIVES AND RELEASE FROM DARKNESS FOR

THE PRISONERS ... AND PROVIDE FOR THOSE

WHO GRIEVE IN ZION — TO BESTOW ON THEM

A CROWN OF BEAUTY INSTEAD OF ASHES, THE OIL OF

GLADNESS INSTEAD OF MOURNING, AND A GARMENT OF

PRAISE INSTEAD OF A SPIRIT OF DESPAIR.

Isaiah 61:1, 3

Since the Fall in the garden of Eden, there have been blue days along life's road, and they aren't always because it's a rainy Monday.

Sometimes we feel like Humpty Dumpty who fell off the wall. We're on the ground, our bodies cracked, our hearts bruised and shattered—and no one around to put us back together.

However, there's good news: God can always put us back together again!

We have a standing reservation for a heart fix when needed at a state-of-the-art heart hospital. The chief surgeon is Jesus, and His main operating instruments are love and the Word.

Even the great prophet Elijah was susceptible to depression. He thought he was the only one left who loved and served God. Elijah ran with his feelings, sat under a tree, and prayed to die. Now that's being down!

God sent an angel to encourage and feed Elijah; and later God Himself came and spoke in that still small voice. He told Elijah that he wasn't the only one—God still had seven thousand servants reserved for Himself. God had come and, with a word, healed Elijah's heart and sent him out again (1 Kings 19).

Whatever blue thoughts or dark situations face you today, come pour God's balm over your wounded heart. Praise and thank Him, in spite of how you feel. That's when healing can begin.

Pastor Don Piper[1] had been in a horrific accident, and was pronounced dead at the scene. Ninety minutes later, he revived miraculously! He writes of his long, painful journey to health for his broken body and soul. Don Piper was constantly in great pain and depressed.

He tells how God healed him from his crushed spirit. Four o'clock one morning, unable to sleep from pain and depressed, he asked a nurse to put a music cassette into the recorder. The first song, "Praise the Lord,"[2] seemed to be saying to him that when you're in a struggle and you think you can't go on, you need to praise the Lord.

Don took these words as from God, and slowly he began to praise the Lord. The tears flowed for over an hour as he praised God. Like a river, the tears came—and eventually God's peace washed away his long-standing depression, giving him a second miracle.

Don still had pounds of stainless steel imprisoning him, but Don's heart had been set free from the chains of sorrow and depression because he had praised the Lord anyway.

Remember, while all the king's horses and all the kings men couldn't put Humpty Dumpty back together again, our King can!

"He heals the brokenhearted and binds up their wounds" (Psalm 147:3).

PRAYER: *Oh God, help me turn to You always when a heaviness tries to rest on my heart. May I know You are the Lord and healer of broken hearts. Help me praise and thank You, no matter what is in my life. Amen.*

Make it yours: Take a few minutes now to praise and thank God for His goodness to you.

Yellow Mind-Set

There will be days that just don't dawn with a smile. However, we can rejoice, because in spite of how it begins, we can turn it into a yellow butterfly day.

Butterflies are beautiful, and they fly high. By faith in the Lord, we are transformed from an ugly, crawling, anchored caterpillar into a beautiful, free, and high flying multi-hued yellow butterfly. The sky is our only limit—and that's just the beginning!

Expressions such as *I'm under the weather* or *I'm just hanging in there* are not butterfly vocabulary. We may be getting older (I hate to tell you, but everyone is) and maybe even wider; we may have an empty nest, or a too full one; we may have a job we don't want, or don't have a job we do want.

Whatever our circumstances, we are not under them. We are flying over—we're the Lord's bright yellow butterfly—and we have all the promises of God as our launch pad.

We should be like my granddaughter, Christine. She just loves the color yellow, thus we've given her the nickname *yellow-girl*. What a color—bright and cheery, with promise—just like her. Let's face each day with a child's mentality—everything is comin' up yellow!

At my local library, I was fascinated looking at a photographic display of butterflies; and they were all yellow. I heard a woman wistfully say to her friend, "Wouldn't you love to start your day looking at these out your window!" I thought to myself, *I can start every day like a yellow butterfly in Christ.*

We don't have to have yellow circumstances; we need a yellow mind-set. Paul and Silas, having been beaten sorely, heavily shackled, and thrown in a dark prison cell, turned that cell yellow with singing and praising God. Their yellow attitude was heard in heaven, and by return mail they received an earthquake of deliverance (Acts 16).

Josephine Campbell of Prince of Peace Church on Long Island, has a bleak record of cancer. She's gone through surgery and remission. The cancer returned, and she now needs ongoing chemotherapy. The constant has been her yellow attitude. She's trusting God to heal her, and while she waits, she serves God and reaches out to others. Josephine sometimes comes to church a little slower, but brings her sweet smile and concern for others—and she's always praising God. Josephine isn't under her circumstances; she's flying high in yellow with God—an inspiration for us all.

We can run through a troop of trouble—scale any mountain that life and the enemy build in front of us. We're more than conquerors with God and His Bible of "Sonshine" yellow promises.

Ask Amy Palmiero-Winters, from Hicksville, New York,[1] what she thinks about being under her circumstances. She is a single mom with two children, training for the Olympic trials. Amy runs sixty to seventy miles a week at a heart pounding twelve miles per hour—and she's an amputee! Now that's a very yellow attitude.

PRAYER: *Lord, whatever comes my way, let me view it as another opportunity to fly over with You. Amen.*

Make it yours: Whatever weighs heavy today, give it to God and praise Him for His solution even though you may not see it yet. Read Isaiah 40:31, and make it personal by putting in your name.

Setting Your GPS

But one thing I do: Forgetting what is behind and
straining toward what is ahead, I press on toward
the goal to win the prize for which God
has called me heavenward in Christ Jesus.

Philippians 3:13 – 14

Today's GPS is a modern marvel, it will map out your
course street by street to your destination. Yet, you still
have to program in your address and follow through by
getting in the car and driving there.

So it is with God, He makes His destination for us
known—which is always north to Him and His will
(Matthew 6:33). However, we have to set our heart and
feet to journey there.

Saul had his default set and followed it with a ven-
geance—until he met Jesus on the Damascus Road.
Jesus then reprogrammed Saul's GPS and set it for the

kingdom of God. Not only a new direction for him, but a new name—Paul (Acts 13:9). He now determined to leave all behind and forge ahead to his goal—the prize of the upward call of God.

As a daughter of God, you aren't afloat like a rowboat without oars in the middle of the ocean. You too are preprogrammed for God and His will. And it is not just for heaven, but for every day until then.

For some, like Solomon, God's will was sky high—the building of the temple. The charge God gave Solomon was: "Now devote your heart and soul to seeking the LORD your God. Begin to build the sanctuary of the LORD God" (1 Chronicles 22:19).

We're not called to build His temple, but whatever our assignment, however humble, it's the same charge for us: devote ourselves to seeking Him. Whatever your age, education, location, or however big or small the assignment, start building.

You're never too young. King Josiah, at eight years old, set his face to walk the road of God's will and brought revival to the land (2 Kings 22).

God called my granddaughter Laura at age eleven to be a missionary. She set her face to follow that road—before she was seventeen she'd been to Bulgaria, Ecuador, and Honduras (where her mother had gone twenty-eight years prior). Now nineteen, Laura is planning another mission trip to Africa.

Don't tell Helen Gustafson, 102 years old, that you are too old. She sought and worked for the Lord all her life—and is still building with what she has. When it was time to retire from a nursing ministry that spanned years and nations (United States, Peru, and Bolivia), she was just taking a breath for another go around.

At eighty-two she ministered as a deaconess and worked with her husband in a rescue mission. Helen was ninety-two when her husband died, then God led her to another ministry. She began visiting and ministering to the "old people" at the healthcare center and still attends church faithfully.[1]

Just as these servants set their face to follow Him—wherever we are, with whatever talents, whatever our age—let's seek Him and His will. Let our hearts cry, as David's did, "Your face, LORD, I will seek" (Psalm 27:8).

PRAYER: *Dear Lord, I seek You and Your will for my life. Lead me to start building for You today in my world. Amen.*

Make it yours: Be on the lookout today for ways to be used for Him.

God Is for Me?

THEN MY ENEMIES WILL TURN BACK WHEN I CALL FOR HELP.
BY THIS I WILL KNOW THAT GOD IS FOR ME.

Psalm 56:9

Superman comics and movies are popular because it's human nature to want someone to guard your back. In a world where fairness and justice don't always prevail, we hope there is a bigger-than-life hero there to save/protect us.

You can walk secure today knowing there's one greater than Superman, one greater than all the world's armies together—and He is for you.

David said he knew God was for him because his enemies had to turn back (Psalm 56:9). We can say the same, and more, for at Calvary the power of the enemy to prevail against us was broken. God is for us, and He proved it by giving His Son: "If [because] God is for us, who can be against us? He who did not spare his own Son, but gave him up for us all—how will he not also, along with him, graciously give us all things?" (Romans 8:31–32).

You may be thinking, "Where's God today—why hasn't He come to my aid yet?" God is for you, whether you think so or not. His timing isn't always ours, but He is never late, and He is always there. If it seems late, you wait, it will be the best answer—for He loves you. We may not have a superhero help us, but God uses ordinary people to show He is for, and with, us.

The movie *Ray*, about singer Ray Charles, shows him as a young child when he first went blind. One day he tripped and was laying on the floor. He cried for his mother to come and help him, and though Ray couldn't see her, she was there. With tears streaming down her face, she silently watched over him until he finally struggled and got up. She knew what Ray wanted, but gave him something much better. She taught him that though he was blind, he could become self-sufficient. Ray Charles was his own answer to prayer, because his mother was for him.[1]

Even as Gideon asked God, if you are for us (which He was) how come all this is happening to us, why are we captives of the Midianites? God answered him in a way that Gideon never expected. In essence, God told Gideon, "I am for you, I am with you, and *you* are going to deliver Israel!" (see Judges 6).

God gives us families as vessels for His help and to mirror His loving faithfulness in being there for us. Ask my eighteen-year-old granddaughter, Laura, who's driving now. She knows as much as most girls at that age know about cars—zero! She'll call from anywhere, at any time and moan, "Dad, the car won't start!" What does Chris say as he's putting on his clothes? "I'll be there; sit tight." Would we dare think Jesus would do any less?

Even if someone doesn't come when you call, if they forsake you as they did Paul—God is there for you! The Lord stood with Paul and strengthened him when everyone left him (2 Timothy 4:16–17).

He'll do the same for you; count on it!

PRAYER: *Dear Lord, thank You that You are for me always. As I go through the day may I think on Your faithful, watchful care and rejoice. Amen.*

Make it yours: Repeat today's title out loud as a statement of fact, instead of as a question—God Is for Me! Look for times during the day when He was there for you. Write it down and thank Him.

Overflowing Hope

MAY THE GOD OF HOPE FILL YOU WITH ALL JOY AND PEACE
AS YOU TRUST IN HIM, SO THAT YOU MAY OVERFLOW WITH
HOPE BY THE POWER OF THE HOLY SPIRIT.

Romans 15:13

For years the *experts* have told us that you can live without many things—but you can't live without hope.

Whenever a terminal diagnosis is given, inevitably the first question is, "Doctor, is there any hope?"

I have great news! You can walk through the unchartered waters of today and tomorrow with your head up high. We are the children of the God of all hope.

"But the eyes of the LORD are on those who fear him, on those whose hope is in his unfailing love" (Psalm 33:18).

Years ago, a friend of mine, Rev. Virginia Bieber, was a single mom raising two children. It was Thanksgiving Day, and she'd promised the children a special dinner.

Virginia could only hope in God to fulfill this promise—for she had nothing except oatmeal, rice, and peanut butter. Ginny's last money had paid the rent with just enough left to get her back and forth to work until the next payday.

She had the kids make decorations and set the table with the good china. She clung to God's promises, meanwhile reminding God it was His part to provide and her part to hope.

Sitting down to the still empty table to read the Bible, her hope began to waver. *I guess I can always heat water for oatmeal or rice*, she thought.

After some time passed, the kids began to fidget and wanted to watch TV or go out and play. Just about deciding to go for the oatmeal, her thoughts were interrupted by a knock on the door.

Two neighbors came in carrying boxes and bags, and began to set them on the table. As the husband went back for more, the wife explained that her husband had been given an elaborate retirement party and all the leftovers had just been delivered! Unfortunately, they were going away!

Everything for a Thanksgiving meal and the rest of the week was there. The only thing missing was milk and eggs.

By the end of the day, God even supplied that. Ginny's friend from downstairs came with a bag of milk, eggs, and butter. She too was leaving town!

Just like Abraham, Ginny had also hoped against all hope. When he and Sarah were beyond childbearing years, they hoped in God for His promise. He answered their hope and faith, as God always does (Romans 4:18).

Whatever is in your life today, or whatever tomorrow may bring, remember—like Abraham and Ginny and everyone who puts their hope in God—you'll not be disappointed.

There's nothing that's impossible with God. Whether it's physical, emotional, spiritual, or other, He is the living God of all hope. He loves you with an unfailing love. He will provide what you need—and then some.

PRAYER: *Oh, Lord, I praise You, and I thank You that You are the God of hope for this day and for tomorrow. Help me to know I will never face a hopeless day, for You are my God of all hope. Amen.*

Make it yours: Whatever in your life may seem hopeless, write it down. Symbolically give it to God and read aloud Romans 15:13 and Psalms 33:18—then determine to believe it.

You're Surrounded!

ARE NOT ALL ANGELS MINISTERING SPIRITS SENT TO
SERVE THOSE WHO WILL INHERIT SALVATION?

Hebrews 1:14

Women generally are the caretakers in life—we are the ones who nurse, protect, nurture, and do the ministering to others. It comes with the territory. Yet, we love to be on the receiving end of this care as well.

I have great news, ladies: we are. We're surrounded! You can't see them, you can't hear them, but they're there for sure. Who are they? None other than God's angels sent to watch over us—and we each have our own personal ones always in the presence of God (Matthew 18:10).

Their job is nothing but to serve and take care of you on God's behalf (don't you just love it?). Next time you're running around, watching over, picking up after, and doing whatever else you have to do, know you're being watched over by heavenly GPAs (God's Protection Agency).

God takes care of us from both sides. God's earthly ministers—the military, the police, the firemen, and other protection agencies—are for our protection too (Romans 13:4). While at times these earthly protection forces can fail, God's heavenly ones never will.

Angels are flying through the Bible from the first pages to the last. There's the story of Elisha's servant arising one morning, finding they were surrounded by a mighty host of Syrian horses and chariots. He fearfully cried to Elisha, "What will we ever do?" Elisha prayed, and asked God to open the servant's eyes—and did He ever! It was more than enough to calm the servant; it was a mountain full of horses and chariots of fire—God's ministering angels (2 Kings 6:14–17).

Then there's Peter, who was sound asleep in jail, and an angel comes, wakes him up, and walks Peter out of prison. This angel had been sent in response to the prayers of God's people (Acts 12).

I've never met an angel, but I have seen one work on my son's behalf. When John David was in his stroller (he's now over thirty)—I was walking fast and furiously trying to make the bank before it closed. The light was red, but there weren't any cars coming, so I continued my pace down the curb. But, what I hadn't seen was a car speeding out of a parking lot, trying to make the light.

I had momentum, as did the unseen car! All of a sudden—it was like the brakes had jammed—the stroller came to a dead stop. The handle slammed hard into my hip, causing me to almost go over the stroller. I looked up to see the car speed by, knowing God had done a miracle! The tears came, for I knew that had the stroller not stopped, John would've been in the direct path of the speeding car. For weeks, every time I looked at the huge black and blue welt on my hip from the handle, I praised God for John's angel watching over him.

So, be encouraged today, because if you could put on fourth dimension glasses, you'd see you're being followed by God's angels. Wherever you go, they go; they're better than having your own Verizon network crew.

PRAYER: *God, I thank You that You watch over me through Your angels. Help me to have peace, knowing You not only love me, but have everything under control. Amen.*

Make it yours: Ask God to reveal to you times when He has watched over you or others. Write them down for future encouragement.

Follow the Leader

SEND FORTH YOUR LIGHT AND YOUR TRUTH,
LET THEM GUIDE ME; LET THEM BRING ME TO YOUR HOLY
MOUNTAIN, TO THE PLACE WHERE YOU DWELL.
THEN WILL I GO TO THE ALTAR OF GOD, TO GOD, MY JOY
AND MY DELIGHT. I WILL PRAISE YOU WITH THE HARP.

Psalm 43:3 – 4

Mapquest and other websites like it that give instant online directions are a modern day wonder. Yet, even these on occasion are known to give wrong information, causing you to end up at the wrong place.

Not so with God. He has given us His Word and the Holy Spirit to guide and lead us in all our ways. We never have to worry about ending up at the wrong destination. The main purpose of God's Word is to lead us to salvation. However, that's just the beginning; He wants to bring us to His holy mountain, into His presence where

He dwells. It's there alone we find the joy and delight we were created for. It is there we find strength and wisdom for the day.

We can get up today knowing we're not a ship without an anchor or a rudder. There's one alongside to make sure we get to the right place, at the right time. Whether it's as big as a move, or as small as what to make for supper—He cares. He says He will give wisdom, and when He says *He will*, He means He will! "I will instruct you and teach you in the way you should go; I will counsel you and watch over you" (Psalm 32:8).

He called Abraham to leave his home and didn't give Him a map, but He made sure Abraham arrived. So, if you are not sure where you are going, just be patient as you wait on God. He'll make sure to get you there on time. Just trust your heavenly GPS, and follow the Leader.

We have a family keepsake photo of my grandson Frankie following hard in the footsteps of his grandfather, Frank, through the park. Without a clue or worry about where his grandfather was going—Frankie just followed him.

We too just have to step out in faith and follow, as did Frankie and the widow Ruth. She turned her back on everyone and everything she had ever known. By faith, she followed God through Naomi's footsteps to the great unknown. What was waiting for her was beyond her wildest dreams! It was in following God's road of wisdom that she found her life of joy and delight (Ruth 1; 4).

God always leads to the mountains—the mountain of His presence, the mountain of wisdom for today and tomorrow—and in His mountains are the ways of light, truth, and joy.

Head for the mountains today!

PRAYER: *Thank You Lord that Your ways are always the roadways of light, truth, and joy. Help me come daily to Your mountain to delight in You. Amen.*

Make it yours: Come rest at His altar today, and spend time enjoying Him. Take the Word, paper, and pen. Ask whatever wisdom you need, and expect an answer. Be patient; it will come.

Honey-Coated Words

PLEASANT WORDS ARE A HONEYCOMB,
SWEET TO THE SOUL AND HEALING TO THE BONES.

Proverbs 16:24

Everyone wants to hear sweet words, especially in the morning. No one wants a cup of vinegar for breakfast. Some days may start with hubby, kids, or boss barking about what happened to the toothpaste, where did you ever put … how could you forget …?

The good news is we always have a sweet word from God: His name is Jesus. God's Word became flesh and dwells among us (John 1:14). He didn't bring us condemnation and vinegar. His Word brings love, life, and healing for crushed souls.

As you start your day filling up on His honey words, you can then bring them wrapped in the unique you, to those around you who are hungry for a good word.

We are God's chosen carriers of soothing, life building words (see Proverbs 12:18).

Just a smile with a cheery hello can make someone's day. When a coworker or a neighbor is down, "I'll be praying for you" can be a real lifter-upper. When we look for it, there's always a good word to shower on someone.

The best thing we can say is what God says about them—*God loves you, God has a good plan for you, God will help you*. And, if appropriate, you can add a touch on their shoulder or hand, and it doubles the impact of the words.

What a blessing to have a sweet word at just that right moment: "A word aptly spoken is like apples of gold in settings of silver" (Proverbs 25:11).

At times you don't even realize how you need a golden apple until you receive it. On a day when I could have used a honeycomb full of words, my twelve-year-old granddaughter Julia left a Post-it stuck on my pulpit: "Hi, Grandma: I love you so, so, much. I hope you have a great day! Julia." And she topped it off with a little red heart!

This not only put a smile on my face, but made my day. I kept the Post-it there for weeks. It's now on my desk at home covered in plastic. This way I can re-eat these words when I'm hungry for some honey.

PRAYER: *Thank You Lord for Your beautiful words to me. Help me determine to speak words of encouragement, healing, and kindness to others. And when*

I can't say anything good, let me say nothing. May I, with Your help, keep a watch over my tongue. With David I pray—"May the words of my mouth and the meditation of my heart be pleasing in your sight" (Psalm 19:14). Amen.

Make it yours: Forgive yourself for words you have said and wished you hadn't. Forgive others for hurtful words they've said to you—and forget. Be on the lookout today, and every day, for someone to speak honeycomb words of life and healing.

What's He Like?

If anyone has ever tried to set you up with a blind date, your first questions usually are: "What's he like, and what's he look like?" This man could be your Mr. Wonderful, and you'll just love everything about him. Eventually though, you might find something you don't like about him (just as he could you).

However, there is someone whom the more you get to know Him, the more you'll love Him. Friends of the Shulammite asked what made her beloved better than another beloved. She responded that the words of his mouth are "sweetness itself, and he's altogether lovely" (Song of Songs 5:9, 16).

What an awesome description; our perfect lover and friend is *altogether lovely*. We will never find something we don't like about Him.

We've all probably told our kids that the best ways to know someone is by listening to what they say and watching what they do. What has our beloved said? In the beginning, He said, "Let there be." And all His *let-there-be's* were to create from nothing a beautiful world for you and me. It was because God loves us and wants us to be with Him.

God is altogether lovely and is your forever friend. Not everyone has a time-tested, faithful, through-it-all, no-matter-what friend. If you have one, as I do in my long time friend, Sue Henke, count it as a big blessing from God. But either way, you have the Friend of friends who will never leave you or forsake you (Hebrews 13:5).

Ruth of the Bible had no children and then her husband died. After his death, Ruth also was going to lose her husband's family, which had been as her own. Her mother-in-law, Naomi, was returning to her homeland and urged Ruth and her sister-in-law to go back to their own pagan families. But Ruth instead chose to make a covenant of friendship with her mother-in-law, and left all she ever knew to follow Naomi to a foreign land.

But Ruth replied, "Don't urge me to leave you or to turn back from you. Where you go I will go, and where you stay I will stay. Your people will be my people and your God my God. Where you die I will die, and there I will be buried. May the LORD deal with me, be it ever so severely, if anything but death separates you and me."

RUTH 1:16–17

In essence, Ruth made a friendship covenant with God; and God was more than faithful to be an altogether lovely friend who more than took care of Ruth and Naomi all the days of their lives.

God the Father, in Christ Jesus, has made an eternal covenant of friendship with us through faith. He was a friend and provider to Ruth, and so He is to us—an altogether lovely forever friend: "Are You not our God, who drove out the inhabitants of this land before Your people Israel, and gave it to the descendants of Abraham Your friend forever?" (2 Chronicles 20:7 NKJV).

PRAYER: *Oh Lord, You have been so very good to me always; thank You for loving me and being my friend. Help me to realize more fully how totally lovely You are. Thank You for being my altogether lovely forever friend. Help me be a faithful friend to You, as Ruth was to Naomi. Amen.*

Make it yours: Take time now to write a list of some of the lovely things God, your friend, has done for you. Read this verse and put your name in place of Abraham's: "'Abraham believed God, and it was credited to him as righteousness,' and he (you) was called God's friend" (James 2:23).

Be looking for an opportunity today to introduce your friend to someone.

Loving Your World

BECAUSE IN THIS WORLD
WE ARE LIKE HIM.

1 John 4:17

Today, whatever the weather is outside, the sun is always shining for you. You're a child of Jesus, the Light of the World. His ways provide an abundance of love, joy, and life (John 10:10). Daily, we can come to Him and take our fill, then go and share it with a world in darkness.

We are His ambassadors, and He has left us big and wide footsteps to follow. His Word is our guide—where we see Jesus doing only good (Acts 10:38). We are to love those who are not easy to love, to give to those who can't give back, to invite those to dinner who can't reciprocate, and more (Matthew 5).

If it were up to you and me, this most likely wouldn't happen. But, the good news is He's in us, and He enables us not only to want to do good—but to do it! (Philippians 2:13).

Jesus' hallmark has always been love. He loved us when we didn't deserve it; He prays for us when we haven't prayed; He gives when we forget to give. And we are to be His agents of this amazing love.

One of the greatest ways we can love the people God has put in our world is to pray for them. We can carry their name to His throne room of grace for salvation, and for anything else they need. We're a royal priesthood, with the privilege of coming before Him on behalf of others (1 Peter 2:9).

What a love message to say to someone, "I prayed for you," or, "What would you like me to pray for you?" That's the pure language of love. These words are hard to fight against.

We don't have to go to Africa to be missionaries of His love; we can do it right where we are. As God asked Moses, "What is that in your hand?" (Exodus 4:2). And God used what Moses had for His world.

Years ago when our cars ran on nothing but faith, whenever they broke down, we'd call my brother John. Wherever he was, he'd soon come with tool box in hand and glue the car back together for yet another round. That's love in action.

A little boy with nothing but five loaves and two small fish gave it to God and He made a miracle of love

(John 6:9). He says whatever we do for someone else is an offering of love to Him (Matthew 25:40).

One of the first contacts I had with Christian love was Donna Falta telling me she was praying for me (and had the whole Bible study doing it besides!). I never knew anyone who prayed, never mind who prayed for me! Then she made me a beautiful green net Christmas angel. Her gospel of love-in-action undid me and opened my heart to the gospel of Christ.

Listen, and you'll hear Him say, "Give them a hug for me." What's in your hand to use for Him today?

PRAYER: *Lord, forgive us for when we haven't loved others for You. Help us to come and take of Your love and then give it away. Amen.*

Make it yours: Write down what's in your hand to love with in His stead—and then do it for Him.

I'm Creative?

THEN GOD SAID, "LET US MAKE MAN
IN OUR IMAGE, IN OUR LIKENESS."
Genesis 1:26

We are made in God's image, and we are like Him, even as a child is like his father. He is the Creator, and He has given unto us the power to create. From the beginning pages of the Bible, God has equipped mankind to create. Adam in the garden had the amazing job of naming every animal and bird. Now that takes creativity! (Genesis 2:19).

God said that the builders of the Tower of Babel could do everything they imagined if He didn't put a stop to what they were planning (Genesis 11:6). God knew man can bring to pass what he puts his mind to do. For good or ill—man has the capacity to create, for we are made in our Creator's image.

You and I are God's agents for creativity in our world. Think of the wonderful things mankind has created and discovered. Whether humans give credit to God or not, it's God who gives all people their abilities: artists, musicians, writers, singers, builders, gardeners, craftsmen, brick layers, tailors, weavers, designers, financiers, and others.

Walt Disney, through the mind God gave him, created Disney World for the world to enjoy. Think of the imagination and innovation it entailed to create it. Disney brought it from an inspired thought into actuality—that's a creator.

The tabernacle and temple of God were magnificent structures built to house the glory of God. God used his people to build it for Him. He is the one who gave each craftsman the wisdom and skill to complete it just as God designed (Exodus 28:3; 36:1).

Whatever our hands find to do—let's be as creative as our Father. Let's look for ways to do things easier, better, and more beautifully. Some people hire experts, or they spend thousands of dollars to glean wisdom from experts in order to learn how to do something. But we have open access to the master creator Himself—God!

And age is no limit to creativity either. Anna Mary Robinson (Grandma Moses) didn't start painting until her mid-seventies when her hands became too arthritic to continue her original embroidery work. Her unique style of folk art is known around the world. Grandma Moses lived to be 101, and in the last year of her life, she painted twenty-five pictures. God gave her a gift she didn't even know she had until she put her hand to a canvas using house paint.[1]

Don Schoendorfer and his wife were in Morocco when they saw a paraplegic woman dragging her useless legs. Her clothes were torn and filthy, and she bled from simply trying to cross the street. This woman, and others like her, who had to claw their way through life, haunted Don. He was an inventor, and decided he wanted to create mobility with dignity for them—and he wanted it to be cheap.

Using the gifts and talents God gave him, Don, through trial and error, created a wheelchair from ordinary plastic lawn chairs and bike tires. The wheelchair is not only durable and able to navigate through the muddy, rocky, dirt roads and trails of poor countries, but it costs only fifty dollars.[2]

Don then founded the Free Wheelchair Mission, which has given hope and mobility to over 300,000 needy people since 2001. That's a man who blessed the world by using God's creative mind in him: "We have the mind of Christ" (1 Corinthians 2:1b).

PRAYER: *Thank You Lord that I am made in Your image. Help me know that as You are the Creator, I too can create. Amen.*

Make it yours: Make a list of something you'd like to do using your individual gifts of imagination and creativity. Then begin in some small way. If you can't think of anything, ask God to give you some ideas. Say out loud, "With God, I can create!" And then start.

Putting up Road Signs

I HAVE BEEN REMINDED OF YOUR SINCERE FAITH,
WHICH FIRST LIVED IN YOUR GRANDMOTHER LOIS
AND IN YOUR MOTHER EUNICE AND,
I AM PERSUADED, NOW LIVES IN YOU ALSO.

2 Timothy 1:5

If you have kids, for sure they've said to you, "I'm watching you!" (probably when you slid through a stop sign, or had a hand in the cookie jar). It comes with the territory—we're always on stage.

God's spiritual giant, Moses, left behind big footsteps. After his death, God told Joshua that He was commissioning Joshua to put on Moses' shoes to lead the people into the land.

Now that's a pair of shoes to fill! Moses lived quite a life on center stage, and he had cast a big shadow. Joshua learned from Moses, but more importantly, Joshua knew the power behind Moses—God.

God let Joshua know that as He was with Moses, so He'd be with Joshua (Joshua 1:5). God is with us too, enabling us to follow the footsteps of His saints, and He makes it possible for us to leave road signs for others.

Paul commended Timothy's faith and credited Timothy's mother and grandmother for passing it on (see above verse). We as women, be it mother, grandmother, aunt, or other, can pass along our faith too. As we walk with the Lord by the power of the Holy Spirit, we'll leave big steps for those behind us to track.

What better gift can we have, and give, than to have our children and grandchildren follow us into the kingdom of God and to serve alongside? It's my husband's and my greatest joy that all our family (and some of the extended family) know the Lord.

At last Christmas' dinner we captured another family-favorite photo and a taste of the legacy one can leave through children. During the saying of grace, Frank is holding our granddaughter Maddie; her hands are folded, her eyes are closed, and her little face is solemn as she prays. It doubles the pleasure, when we hear both Maddie and her twin brother Zach enthusiastically singing their Sunday school praises to Jesus.

We all have the awesome privilege of walking and working for the Lord, and the added benefit of knowing we're influencing others. God doesn't call us to be perfect (He's the only perfect one), but to be faithful in our love for Him. Our feet will follow our heart, and others will follow us.

May God inspire us with the desire and will to leave an enduring charge to our family and those around us to love and follow the Lord all the days of their lives (Mark 12:29–31), even as David did:

> And you, my son Solomon, acknowledge the God of your father, and serve him with wholehearted devotion and with a willing mind, for the LORD searches every heart and understands every motive behind the thoughts. If you seek him, he will be found by you; but if you forsake him, he will reject you forever.

> 1 CHRONICLES 28:9

PRAYER: *Dear Lord, thank You that we can touch those around us for You. Help us to stay close to You that we may walk in Your ways, thereby leaving a bright heavenward trail. May it not only be by our words, but by our deeds and actions that they would see You and desire to follow. Amen.*

Make it yours: Think of someone you can influence for the kingdom. Pray that God would use you to inspire them to love and pursue God and His ways.

Open Door Policy

I SLEPT BUT MY HEART WAS AWAKE. LISTEN!
MY LOVER IS KNOCKING: "OPEN TO ME, MY SISTER,
MY DARLING, MY DOVE, MY FLAWLESS ONE."

Song of Songs 5:2

An open door is an international welcome sign saying, *come on in*. Before God came and knocked on the closed door of our hearts for salvation, our lives were a closed door to Him. However, after salvation, God desires that we keep an open door policy to Him.

Daily, He stands knocking at our door; and He softly whispers that we are *His sister, His darling, His dove, and His flawless one!* What an inducement to open to Him! Though we have been sleeping, He bids us come by words of endearment—what a lover!

With our heart open and waiting, He enters; we walk and talk, we learn of Him, we become like Him.

The open door is also the way to receive His blessings. We don't want to miss anything, as did the Shulammite woman, because we're sleeping, or our door is closed tight, or we take too long to open (Song of Songs 5:6).

With joy of anticipation, let's leave our door open for His fellowship and His blessings. What treasures await those who abide with Him and keep an open-heart policy (Psalm 91).

Our lover even challenges us to test Him in the area of His blessings. As we give to Him, He will pour back through our open door:

> "Bring the whole tithe into the storehouse, that there may be food in my house. Test me in this," says the LORD Almighty, "and see if I will not throw open the floodgates of heaven and pour out so much blessing that you will not have room enough for it."
>
> MALACHI 3:10

The greatest blessings are beyond what He materially gives (though they are most wonderful, and He wants us to enjoy them). His inner circle, Peter, James, and John, always had an open door policy to the Lord. They're the ones who knew His heart, His ways, and His secrets—they saw Jesus in His glory, beheld Moses and Elijah, and heard the voice of the Father! (Matthew 17). As we dwell with Him, we too will see His glory (John 17:22)!

When we answer His gentle knock and open the door to Him, He comes in and overcomes us with His beauty and love. We take and we take, for it's His pleasure to give.

Looking at our hands, we'll see from opening the door, they are dripping with the fragrance of His heavenly myrrh left on the latch. It is for us to enjoy and to bring and share with a hungry world (Song of Songs 5:5).

When Peter saw Jesus walking on the water, Peter told Jesus, "Call me and I will come." Jesus called Peter, and he walked on water (Matthew 14:28–29). However, when we open our door and call Him to come—we walk on the heavenly waters sharing in His glory.

PRAYER: *Oh Lord, let me not be satisfied with an earthbound walk. Help me hunger and thirst for a heavenly encounter and walk with You. You promised that as I thirst, rivers of water would flow within and out from me. I open my door and ask You to come in. Help me to keep a doorstop under the open door daily. Amen.*

Make it yours: Determine each day to have an open door and to walk the upper highway with Him.

Evergreen Faith

Green may not be your best color, but God loves to see you in it. Green symbolizes growing faith, which means we need to fertilize and water it by exercise. Let's aim for brilliant green. Today, in fact, let's attempt to be the Jolly Green Giant of faith.

Even a child, in the face of obstacles, can grow faith green and greener. My grandson John was diagnosed with Perthes disease of the hip at seven. It's not life threatening, however it's a major life-changer. The doctors said John needed several surgeries, and would never walk normally again—and he'd never play baseball.

However, they didn't take into consideration the power of a boy who dared to believe God.

John loved baseball passionately and had been one of the team's best players and fastest runners. After two operations, he maneuvered around on crutches, eventually walking with a limp. Throughout, he still continued to practice throwing baseballs and never considered he wouldn't play again.

After John's recovery he still ran clumsily, but he'd seen too many answers to prayer. And in the middle of the season, with the encouragement of his coach and family, he returned to baseball. He had opportunities to give up; however, his faith didn't give up.

During his first game, John hit the ball and bit by bit ran to first base. Finally, arriving on base, the first baseman said, "It sure took you long enough!"

John replied, "I got here. You don't have the ball, and I'm safe!"

Unbeknownst to John, this never-give-up-kid who believed God, would once again be back on this same field. Except, this time, it would be as part of a hand-picked all-star team, and he'd make the blazing final play. Now that's green giant faith!

Maybe you're way beyond being young, like Nola Ochs[1] who graduated college and is considering a master's degree—and she's ninety-five! Or as Anna, who by faith served God in the temple night and day. Her fertile faith was rewarded by having her eyes behold the One who Israel looked to for their redemption (Luke 2:36–38).

Today, most likely you're not playing baseball or starting college. Nonetheless, you'll have opportunity to increase your faith. And if not today, then tomorrow.

Maybe it's a troublesome neighbor or coworker that'll help grow your faith. Or maybe it will be a job interview. Perhaps, it's starting an exercise program, or another attempt at weight loss, or stretching your budget into black when it's shocking bright red.

Whatever it is, you can grow greener than a garden having had a double dose of MiracleGro. Put your hand in God's hand, the Father of giants, and walk by faith with your feet anchored on the evergreen promises of God. Soon you'll be a dazzling green giant.

PRAYER: *Lord, thank You for the seed of faith You've given me. Help me to fertilize and grow it by trusting You and Your promises, no matter what I see. Amen.*

Make it yours: Find a promise for your situation and grow it green with the water and sunshine of your faith.

The Real You

YOUR EYES SAW MY UNFORMED BODY.
ALL THE DAYS ORDAINED FOR ME WERE WRITTEN IN
YOUR BOOK BEFORE ONE OF THEM CAME TO BE.

Psalm 139:16

Years ago there was a fad called "Come-as-you-are-party." Ahead of time, you agreed that when you were called, you'd come just as you were. (If you were in underwear, you could put on pajamas.) The reason I think these parties didn't last long was the girls never really came as they were—which was obvious when they arrived.

At times we do that with God. We think we have to look, act, or do right before we can come to Him. Some women think He doesn't love them unless they're up to par in certain areas.

The good news is He loves us just the way we are. The *real you* is not the one looking at us from the mirror.

The *real you* is the inner woman—the one made in the image of God, the one we are growing into.

"Therefore we do not lose heart. Though outwardly we are wasting away, yet inwardly we are being renewed day by day" (2 Corinthians 4:16).

We are God's unique child. He looks not only at what we are today, and loves us anyway, but He knows what we will become under His gentle tutelage, just as a parent sees the yet untested and untrained potential within a child. They look at his/her childish ways, and by faith see down life's road what their child will become.

God looked beyond Gideon's fears and doubts and called Gideon "a mighty man of valor." God saw the untapped possibilities in Gideon and gave him the job of delivering the Israelites. Their enemy, the Midianites, were overpowering in numbers, training, and strength, However, Gideon with God alongside, defeated them with only three hundred untrained, unequipped men! Now that was the real Gideon, not the one hiding in a cave from the enemy (Judges 6–7).

Growing into what God created us for will include taking some missteps and making some messes. However, that's what children do: we make mistakes as we grow up. In spite of our sins, He loves us and doesn't condemn (while not condoning outright sin). We belong to God, and He already knows that with Him alongside, we are going to arrive at His beautiful, preplanned destination for us. Anne Sullivan[1] was a woman who saw beyond the handicaps of Helen Keller's blindness, deafness, severely limited speech, and undisciplined ways. Armed with faith, love, perseverance, and knowledge, Anne lead Helen Keller beyond her limitations to become the *real* Helen—a Helen who reflected the love and limitless power of God's potential to be all you can and was a living example to all the world.

> PRAYER: *Thank You Lord, that You love me as I am. And You look beyond my mistakes and see what I will become as I yield to Your powerful loving hand. I praise You that You will gently guide me along Your path to becoming all I am created for—a woman reflecting Your glory in my world, for that is the real me. Help me not limit myself by what I see today. Amen.*

Make it yours: Spend some time today with the Lord and ask Him to reveal where you have been perhaps quenching God's *real you*. Then read the above Psalm 139:16 again, and determine to follow God's plan for the ongoing unfolding of the inward you.

Songs of Deliverance

YOU ARE MY HIDING PLACE;

YOU WILL PROTECT ME FROM TROUBLE AND

SURROUND ME WITH SONGS OF DELIVERANCE.

Psalm 32:7

We've all seen children cover their eyes and say, "Find me." Like an ostrich, they naively think if they can't see you, you can't see them. If only it were so easy! Sometimes there'll be days we may want to hide our heads in the sand. However, we know better than to think covering our eyes will do it.

Maybe your mother-in-law is coming to stay for six months, or someone has stolen your identity, or perhaps your kids aren't getting with the program. Whatever it is, you can face it head on with His song in your heart: "I will put you in a cleft in the rock and cover you with my hand … and you will see [me]" (Exodus 33:21–23).

We can all identify with David in Psalm 55, who walked with God, who loved and served Him and yet at times wanted to bolt. He cried out to God in fear and trembling: if he only had the wings of a dove, David would fly to a place for shelter from his storm. However, David came to what he already knew was his answer, and God has left it for us. He said, "But as for me, I trust in you." All David had to do was head to his hiding place—God—where once again David would hear God's song of deliverance (Psalm 55:16–23).

Some people find comfort in the thought of going on vacation to get away from things at home. However, when they come back the things left behind are still waiting. But, when we go to God for our deliverance, He enables us to be strengthened for the task or to go around it. All the while we can whistle our happy victory song, for He is with us.

One day Daniel's three friends found themselves thrown in the fiery furnace. On the way down God sang sweet songs of deliverance. When their feet hit bottom, in the midst of that fire, they opened their eyes, and it became their hiding place!

Whatever unfolds today, or is left over from yesterday, you don't have to hide under the covers. You can jump out of bed and go to His throne room where He is waiting. Feel His arms around you, and relax in the power of His love. Put on your heavenly headphones and rejoice listening to His sweet song of deliverance just for you: "The LORD your God is with you, he is mighty to save. He will take great delight in you, he will quiet you with his love, he will rejoice over you with singing" (Zephaniah 3:17).

> PRAYER: *Oh Lord, praise You for Your songs of deliverance over me. Open my ears that I might hear clearly Your sweet quieting songs of loving, watchful care. May Your tune capture my heart and mind. Help me remember to sing it throughout my days. Thank You Lord. Amen.*

Make it yours: Read out loud Psalm 32:7. Start to memorize it. Be on the lookout for someone who needs to hear it today.

Power of One

AND WHO KNOWS BUT THAT YOU HAVE COME
TO ROYAL POSITION FOR SUCH A TIME AS THIS?

Esther 4:14

Queen Esther woke one day never knowing before the sun went down that God would present her with a super-sized divine assignment. By faith Esther rose to the call and with a God-inspired plan she saved her people from extinction.

Tomorrow may start out ordinary for you and become extraordinary when God comes to visit. We're called to our corner of the world for such a time as this. Today, we can turn our world upside down for someone or begin a work to turn it right side up.

Joshua was a great military leader, and war was his forte. Yet one day, after having a visit with God, Joshua did beyond what any military leader or any man has ever done before, or since. Joshua spoke to the sun and moon to stand still—and they obeyed! Now that's the power of one with God (Joshua 10:12–14).

George Washington Carver was born a slave in 1864, and before he died he accomplished more than many do in several lifetimes. He was a man who walked with God, and is quoted as asking God to reveal the mystery of the universe. God told him *no*, but said He would reveal secrets of the peanut to George!

God used him to develop over three hundred products from peanuts and more than a hundred from the sweet potato. George Washington Carver helped establish the Tuskegee Institute which became one of the leading schools of higher learning for African Americans.[1]

These are only a few things that George Washington Carver accomplished—the power of one with God!

There are still things to be discovered, invented, and accomplished. Matthew Barnett felt a call of God to start a church where there was a need. He left the comfort of suburban Phoenix, Arizona, and his father Pastor Tommy Barnett's church. Stepping out with faith and a God-dream, with his father's help, and through one miracle after another, Matthew began the Dream Center in Los Angeles.

This has become the prototype of ministry for others throughout the world. By faith and hard, dirty work, Dream Center has grown from ministering to forty-eight people to over thirty-five thousand hurting souls. The town the church was in was famous for gangs, drug and alcohol addiction, prostitution, homelessness, and hopelessness, so much so that people would drive around this seemingly forsaken area rather than drive through it.

Since Matthew's ministry started, violence has dropped 73 percent, murders 28 percent, rapes 53 percent. The impact is so evident that the mayor has publicly acknowledged and praised this ministry.

It's called Dream Center because Matthew wanted to give people the opportunity through God to dream again. His God-thinking is, "Find a need and fill it, find a hurt and heal it."[2]

Throughout our day, may we have this God mindset. Let's find a need, and fill it on the spot, or prayerfully start plans for a long range cure. The power of one—with God!

PRAYER: *Lord, awaken in me a dream so big that only You could do it. May I, like Gideon, Esther, and Matthew Barnett, love the people enough to put my hand to the plow—knowing You will complete the dream You put in my heart. Amen.*

Make it yours: Be praying, looking, and writing down ways God can use you—and begin to bring it to pass.

High-Stepping in the Spirit

SINCE WE LIVE BY THE SPIRIT,
LET US KEEP IN STEP WITH THE SPIRIT.
Galatians 5:25

Most sports have a coach who is able to see the bigger picture of the game that is being played. Therefore during a game, with their experience and vantage point, they are able to give timely directions to the players concerning things they do not see. When the players heed the instructions of the coach, they are in a better position to win. When they don't follow the coach's directions, it can mean someone getting hurt, or an advantage for the other team, or the loss of the game. When we say *yes* to God's gift of salvation, He gives us the gift of Holy Spirit as our divine coach. He sets us on His high road where we can walk side by side with Him and follow the just-for-us trail He has mapped out. As we set our steps by the Holy Spirit's pace and agree on His predetermined destination, we are assured of a glorious journey.

The catechisms of the Christian faiths agree on what that heavenly mapped-out trip is: "The chief end of man is to glorify God, and to *enjoy Him forever*."[1]

What a life itinerary—glorifying God and enjoying Him, starting this minute and every day throughout forever! Traveling hand-in-hand with Him, we can avoid the detours, the wash outs, and the accidents, and we can whistle a happy traveling tune, dodging landmines along the way.

Any terrain is conquerable without concern when we have advance info from the Holy Spirit and the Word. He gives us hourly updates on where the enemy's traps are. We can jog through the warzone avoiding landmines such as fear, pride, unforgiveness, jealousy, etc. If we fall out of sync with the Holy Spirit, it means we have taken our eyes off His official guidebook for our trail; as the Bible says, how can two walk the same road unless they agree? (Amos 3:3).

If we miss a turn, or take a detour, He's waiting to forgive, dust us off, and put us back on His road.

Coming often to the heavenly headquarters, we can be privy to the Master's plan for our pathway of life. We will leave with our senses sharpened to hear His voice. Even as Elijah took a detour, parked under a tree, and then proceeded to complain about the journey, God showed up, not in an earthquake or in a fire, but in a gentle whisper, and recommissioned Elijah and put him on God's road again. Elijah once again was in sync with the Spirit's steps (1 Kings 19:4–18).

There's no greater call and privilege than to walk in step with the Spirit on our journey home. It is here we have the power and confidence to accomplish greater things for the kingdom (Ephesians 3:20). It is with the Holy Spirit in control of our hearts and lives that we have an overflow of love, joy, peace, longsuffering, kindness, goodness, faith, gentleness, and self-control (Galatians 5:22–23), with leftovers for others.

Now that's the high-stepping road home!

PRAYER: *Thank You Father, for sending the Holy Spirit to empower me to know and to do Your will. May I walk with You today and enjoy You. Keep me by Your side. Amen.*

Make it yours: Say, "My purpose in life is to walk in the Holy Spirit and to enjoy God." Repeat it throughout the day—and then do it.

Thanksgiving Surround

ALWAYS GIVING THANKS TO GOD THE FATHER FOR
EVERYTHING, IN THE NAME OF OUR LORD JESUS CHRIST.

Ephesians 5:20

Being thankful is in vogue since experts have found it's good for us. However, God told us that long before there were any experts.

For most of us, it's not difficult being thankful and content when things are going well—but God calls us to thankfulness always, and that can be hard sometimes.

Perhaps today in your life, or the life of a loved one, there is something that makes contentedness and thankfulness difficult. You aren't alone; life and the Bible are filled with people struggling with thankfulness in the midst of trying situations.

Joseph had reasons not to be thankful; his brothers were jealous, they planned to kill him, but in their greed, they sold him into slavery instead. Joseph then worked for Potiphar as a high ranking slave. Potiphar's wife lied and had Joseph thrown in prison for resisting evil. More testing was to come, yet Joseph learned contentedness and thankfulness (Genesis 37–42).

Once in a while a person crosses our path, and we get a picture of what thankfulness truly means. Such is remarkable, handsome, twenty-two year old Nick Vugicic of Australia.[1] From birth he has dealt with a handicap that would have put lesser men under. He's not only content and thankful, but tells anyone who'll listen how God is so good, and that we have everything needed to be thankful—God.

This is a man whose mother at his birth could only say, "Please take him away!" Why? He was healthy, but had neither arms or legs, just one foot with a few toes, attached to his torso. His Christian parents had their faith sorely tested. However, God gave grace upon grace in their great trial of faith (2 Corinthians 12:8–10).

Nick grew up surrounded by his loving and supportive family. He amazingly went to regular school where he learned the aloneness of being handicapped. Nonetheless, God was with Nick and used it to strengthen and prepare him for a powerful future ministry.

Nick learned thankfulness, because God told Nick He would never leave him or forsake him (Hebrews 13:5).

At times Nick was discouraged and angry with God. At

one low point, he couldn't see any hope or future for himself. God, through the Word, gave Nick the revelation that there indeed was a hope and future for him. He showed Nick that when we suffer, God strengthens us—drawing us closer to Him—and that we always find Him when we seek Him with all our heart (Jeremiah 29:11–14).

Ever since, Nick has done just that—sought hard after God with thankfulness.

Nick graduated college with a double degree. He's able to write using a special attachment on his toes, and types better than many able bodied people. Living in his parents' specially equipped house, he's decidedly independent and takes care of his own needs.

God has led him into an ever-growing worldwide speaking ministry. He especially loves ministering to youth, to whom he tells the secret of contentment and thankfulness: God with us, through whom we can do all things (Philippians 4:13).

Watching Nick's infectious joy, thankfulness, and optimism causes us to say, "So, what's my problem?"

PRAYER: *Lord, forgive me for being unthankful. Help me daily to be thankful for all You do for me. Amen.*

Make it yours: Make a list of all the things for which you're thankful—and thank God for them. Tell someone today how thankful you are.

More Than a Conqueror?

Let's pretend we're in Jerusalem approximately two thousand years ago, and the local radio station announces a special bulletin:

> We're interrupting regular broadcasting with an amazing story! His empty tomb has been verified by over five hundred eyewitnesses—Jesus Christ has risen from the dead—just like He said in a recent interview. What does that mean?
>
> Let me tell you: Jesus said He would conquer sin and death, and He accomplished it on our very own Calvary Hill! More good news—He did it for you, and now you're more than a conqueror! Some listeners will call in and ask, "What's more than a

conqueror?" Tune in tomorrow, and we'll give the latest on that. Till then—walk like a conqueror.

Today, it's still the best news. Jesus took the penalty, rose again to conquer sin and death, then gave us the benefits without the pain.

A beautiful picture of this shined from the blackness of the Auschwitz death chambers in 1941. A prisoner had escaped, and the Nazis chose ten prisoners to die by starvation in reprisal. One of the men chosen to die began to cry out, "My wife! My children! I will never see them again!" Father Kolbe, moved with compassion for the man, stepped forward and asked to die in his place. Surprisingly, he was not killed on the spot, and his request was granted; Franciszek Gajowniczek lived; in his place, Father Kolbe died a slow, painful death of dehydration and starvation.[1]

We are not only a conqueror over death through Christ. Today and tomorrow, whatever's in your path, you're victorious—more than a conqueror. Maybe the walls of Jericho are surrounding you. God says, "I've given it to you—take it. Come, wait for my directions. Stand and watch them tumble at your feet" (see Joshua 6).

Perhaps you have the wall of a bad habit holding you captive. Maybe jealousy consumes you—someone's house, husband, looks, money, job, etc. No one knows (or so you think), but it's killing you. It may even be affecting you physically (Proverbs 14:30).

Perhaps it's legal medication, alcohol, food, or drugs. Don't let shame keep you in bondage. You have Jesus the ladder, who came to set the captives free by faith, so climb to your freedom. You have all God's arsenal to conquer whatever it is; repentance, faith, and the sword of the spirit. Pick them up, and watch the walls collapse.

Jesus said that *all* things are possible if you believe (Mark 9:23). The Shunammite woman is an example of this conquering faith. She asked God for a miracle of a son. God had compassion, honored her faith, and granted her request. The child grew, but one day he became sick and died.

She was asked twice if everything was okay (by those who didn't know yet the child was dead). Her answer: "It is well!" Her victorious, more-than-a-conqueror faith in God kept her walking to her miracle. God answered, and her son lived again (2 Kings 4:18–37).

PRAYER: *Thank You Lord, I'm more than a conqueror through Your victory on Calvary. Help me by faith to walk in it. Reveal if there's anything that holds me too tight. Amen.*

Make it yours: Write down what God reveals to you. Determine today to repent, and be set free. Ask a trusted mature Christian to pray with you. Declare with faith: "I'm more than a conqueror!"

Magnificent Obsession

O GOD, YOU ARE MY GOD, EARNESTLY I SEEK YOU;
MY SOUL THIRSTS FOR YOU, MY BODY LONGS FOR YOU, IN A
DRY AND WEARY LAND WHERE THERE IS NO WATER.

Psalm 63:1

Within every woman beats a God-shaped heart. Over the door hangs a sign that says, *Reserved for Creator.* We were created for Him—anything less than His love filling and ruling our life won't completely satisfy. God wants us longing for Him in the midst of the pulls on our heart.

Women sometimes expect too much from men because of their deep need for love, security, and intimacy. Eventually she'll be disappointed when he falls short, as we all do. We were made for Him; everything and everyone else, no matter how wonderful, will fall short.

Such a woman was Leah. Leah was Jacob's first wife,

but not his first love. What disappointment and rejection must have stabbed Leah when Jacob woke up and freaked because she wasn't Rachel—the one he loved. Leah had dull eyes and probably lived in the shadow of her sister Rachel's beauty her whole life. Now, Leah had to live with being the unwanted bride.

While Leah desperately sought Jacob's love, God was wooing and calling Leah to find true love in Him. Rachel had Jacob's heart, but a closed womb. Because Leah was unloved, God opened her womb (Genesis 29:31). In their culture a woman's value and divine favor was measured by how many children she could birth, especially male children.

Leah was of great worth to God, and He gave her four sons.

Through the naming of Leah's children, we see her journey of seeking Jacob's heart turn into finding God's. Leah named her first child Reuben, *The Lord sees*, and she hoped her husband would now love her (Genesis 29:32). She believed God gave a second son, Simeon, because she was unloved (v. 33). When Levi was born, Leah still sought Jacob's love; she looked for him to become attached to her, now that she had three sons (v. 34).

At the birth of her fourth son, Leah came to true love. This time she didn't seek Jacob's heart, but praised the one who loved her totally—the one to whom she was everything. Leah named him Judah, meaning *praise*; I will now praise the lover of my soul—God (v. 35).

Leah had been obsessed with seeking Jacob's love, and in not obtaining it, she found her magnificent obsession—the one who loved her more than a million Jacobs ever could; the one to whom she was the apple of His eye; the one who called her to the inner chamber and called her beautiful (Song of Songs 1:4; 6:4). Leah was the beloved bride of the bridegroom, just as you are today.

"For your Maker is your husband—the LORD Almighty is his name" (Isaiah 54:5).

Today, whatever your thoughts are about a husband, you have one. There is none like Him. He says to you, "You're always on my mind. Hunger for me, seek me as water when you are thirsty. I wait for you. Come—I chose you as my bride, not for what you do or how you look, but because I love you. Can you not love me because I first loved you?" (See Psalms 139:17–18; 63:1; Deuteronomy 7:7–8; 1 John 4:19.)

PRAYER: *Dear lover of my soul, help me respond to Your call of love. May I make You my magnificent obsession. Amen.*

Make it yours: Find a suitable psalm and make it a love song to God, or take today's verse and make it yours.

While You Wait

I WAIT FOR THE LORD, MY SOUL WAITS, AND IN HIS WORD
I PUT MY HOPE. MY SOUL WAITS FOR THE LORD.

Psalm 130:5 – 6

No one likes to wait, yet life seems to be filled with hold-ups and delays.

It's no different in our Christian walk; we want to be giant Christians instantaneously, doing great things. God sends a dream, we look in tomorrow's mail for it. Instead we're anchored in God's waiting room.

God gave Joseph a dream (Genesis 37). It took approximately thirteen years until the jailor opened Joseph's prison door. It wasn't man who kept Joseph's dream from coming to pass, it was God! When God was finished with Joseph — the dream started in Technicolor. Meanwhile Joseph served and waited (Psalm 105:17 – 22).

William Carey, the father of Protestant missions, is

a neon example of waiting on the Lord. William said, "Expect great things; attempt great things." While he waited, he said, "I can plod for God." In 1792, he organized a missionary society and went to India. William and his family suffered great hardships of health, finances, and loneliness. He wrote, "This is indeed the valley of the shadow of death to me. But, I rejoice that I am here notwithstanding; and God is here."

Upon Carey's death, after forty-one years, there were only seven hundred converts among millions. However, while he waited, he'd accomplished Bible translations, great educational and social reforms, and laid the foundation for worldwide missionary movements that inspired many thousands (such as Adoniram Judson, Hudson Taylor, and David Livingston).[1]

William Carey didn't wait in vain—no one who waits on God waits in vain.

Since grade school I desired to write. My first writer's conference wasn't until 1980 (I was 38). There I met Marlene Bagnull, already into her writing career, who took time to encourage me and give me direction for publication. For years as I waited, I prayed and learned the craft, getting some articles published. Twenty-seven years later, I have an agent and a published book!

My son Frank is called to ministry. For now, he's seated in God's waiting room. One day, Frank too will hear God's call from the waiting room, and His God-dream will begin. Meanwhile, as Frank waits, he prepares and serves, as in a recent mission trip to Cuba.

God promised Simeon He wouldn't die until he saw the Christ. Simeon waited many years until one day he held the Messiah in his own hands! (Luke 2:26).

My daughter, Maria Elena, at eight years old, sang Psalm 19 with a friend. As she sang, God moved me to pray that she'd one day sing for the Lord (that was thirty-six years ago!). While waiting on God to open more doors, she's had throat problems and other disappointments. She has the call, the desire, the talent, and the touch of God—meanwhile she waits. As she waits she leads in praise and worship.

For years, God's people have been praying and fasting for revival rains. We should never give up. It will come—faint not! Meanwhile, we keep praying, and while we wait let's be looking out the window for rain.

Be patient sitting in God's waiting room—in the interim, believe, work, and pray.

PRAYER: *Lord, help me revive the dreams You've given me, and then wait on You. You are the fulfiller of dreams, and those who wait on You will not be disappointed. Amen.*

Make it yours: Write down what you have been waiting on God for, and write the above verse over it—then be patient!

The Worthy Walk

AND WE PRAY THIS IN ORDER THAT YOU MAY LIVE A LIFE
WORTHY OF THE LORD AND MAY PLEASE HIM IN EVERY WAY:
BEARING FRUIT IN EVERY GOOD WORK.

Colossians 1:10

You are royalty—your Father is the King of Kings! With your royalty comes the call to live worthy of the family name. The French phrase *noblesse oblige* expresses it well—"Honorable and generous behavior is considered the responsibility and obligation of persons of high birth."[1]

That's our call—to walk worthy of Him—to love Him with all our heart, soul, mind, and strength; and our neighbors as ourselves (Mark 12:29–31). We live a worthy high call when we love Him more than anything, and from this flows love and service to others.

His love is so compelling, has such a draw on us—it

creates the passion to love, follow, and serve. He's inde-scribable—His love so incomparable—it's easy to love Him above all else! Anything we give up is nothing com-pared to what He has given.

This love woos us to daily deny ourselves and follow (Luke 9:23). In yielding, we turn from self; we find total satisfaction and our greatest treasure—God.

Throughout the ages people have willingly left all to follow Him. They have heeded the call: "Listen, O daughter, consider and give ear: Forget your people and your father's house" (Psalm 45:10).

Ruth Graham tells the story of a young man in 1920 who'd found God worthy of all and went to China as a missionary. An oil company started a new operation in China and felt because of this man's education and knowledge of the people and language, he was perfect to work as a liaison for their oil company.

His mission board paid him $600 a year, and the oil company offered him $10,000 to take the job. When he refused, they offered $15,000; he turned it down too. When asked how much it would take, he answered, "It's not a question of salary. The salary is tremendous. The trouble is the job—it's too little. I feel God has called me to preach the Gospel of Christ. I'd be a fool to quit preaching in order to sell oil." Now, that's a man who denied himself and picked up his cross.[2]

We don't have to move to China to bear fruit for

Him. Sometimes it means passing up or leaving a job for conscience's sake, or not moving on up when given the opportunity.

At times, it's hardest to walk worthy in our own homes; denying ourselves the spouting of hurtful, angry, or judgmental words. It's not always easy to walk in love, but we have the Spirit to enable us to overcome by His love, thereby bearing kingdom fruit and pleasing Him.

Living worthy has no age limit—even children are given the opportunity. My nephew Stephen was into collecting Pokemon cards. When he realized these cards were a doubtful activity for a Christian, and a possible stumbling block to his friends, he packed them up and put them away in his attic. Now, that's living worthy of the Lord—at nine years old!

PRAYER: *Lord, help me to walk worthy of You today. Show me in what areas I need to yield and follow Your promptings. Thank You for the Spirit to help me. Amen.*

Make it yours: Meditate on Colossians 1:9–14. Write down what it says to you and share it with someone.

Keep on Praying

So I say to you: Ask and it will be given to you;
seek and you will find; knock and the door
will be opened to you. For everyone who asks receives;
he who seeks finds; and to him who knocks,
the door will be opened.

Luke 11:9 – 10

Being a pain-in-the-neck or aggressively bold aren't traits often admired. However, there's a time for everything; and when you want something—really want something—that's a time to keep-on-keeping-on (kids are masters at it). If you're legitimately owed one million dollars, how persevering would you be until you received it?

God loves persistence and boldness in prayer. Whenever someone went to God and asked and asked—they received. There was a Canaanite woman who came and asked Jesus to help her suffering daughter. Jesus didn't answer; the disciples urged Him to send her away because she kept after them. Jesus finally answered and said, "Your people aren't the ones to whom I was sent."

This woman still didn't give up—she had the nerve to ask again! Jesus then told her the healing bread was for the Jew (which she wasn't). Talk about being rejected—it's four times now! She didn't give up, and said that even the dogs ate of the crumbs under the table. Now that's faith!

Jesus was impressed with her persistent faith and granted her request; all because she kept on asking. If she had not persevered and pressed in—she wouldn't have received her answer. She was bold—very bold—and God commended her! (Matthew 15:21–28).

Has it been years you've been praying for a prodigal, or for your yet-to-be-saved kids, parents, hubby, or grandkids, and you wonder, *will this ever happen*? Keep on praying.

Sue Henke, my best friend and fellow minister, prayed for her mom for over thirty-five years. She could have given up; her mom was ninety-one now. Well, Sue's patience in prayer paid off—Peg Ryder is now ninety-three and making up for lost time.

For years, Sue also waited and prayed for her husband Chuck, and finally he was saved. But she wanted more, and for more years continued to pray for him to sit next to her in church. Guess who's next to her now, making us all crazy—Chuck!

Perhaps you've prayed for a lost loved one whose heart seems as stone. God tells you to keep on asking and expecting. It will come. Jesus told the disciples that it was harder for a camel to go through the eye of a needle, than for a rich man to get saved. They were aghast and asked—how then can anyone get saved? His reply was—with man it is impossible, but with God all things are possible.

I'll paraphrase that for you—God says, "a person's heart can be so blinded by riches, the cares of life, or sin that they can't see me. But, I can take any heart and make it into a heart of flesh that will see clearly and will therefore desire me" (see Luke 18:23–27).

Help Him out—keep on praying!

PRAYER: *Oh, Lord, help me to keep praying with a passion that won't let go, and not to give up until You answer. Amen.*

Make it yours: Write down on a piece of paper today's verse. Underneath put the prayer requests or the person's salvation you have been seeking for such a long time. Now pray with the tenacity of faith that never gives up!

Investment Portfolio

BEHOLD, I AM COMING SOON!
MY REWARD IS WITH ME, AND I WILL GIVE
TO EVERYONE ACCORDING TO WHAT HE HAS DONE.

Revelation 22:12

Workers for the kingdom of God never have to worry about their pensions. What happened to Enron employees, whose retirement funds were gone like feathers in the wind, will never happen to us. Our future retirement investments are held in the accounts of heaven—where no thief can ever touch or any moth destroy (Luke 12:32–34).

Our rewards will never greedily be gobbled up by someone, and the accounting's never tied up by inefficiency and red tape. What we send on is secure and insured by God Himself!

Moses was a man who knew a good investment

move when he saw it. He turned from everything Pharaoh's house had to offer and started a future investment portfolio. He left behind rewards of godless living, with its riches and prestige, to start working for the unseen kingdom, but with sure rewards. Moses now lives forever with the fruit of his labor! (Hebrews 11:25–26).

Eric Liddell, an Olympic runner, turned down the fame and rewards of athletics to put his hands to the kingdom plow and never looked back. With joy Eric walked through hardships of ministering in China; meanwhile he kept depositing into his heavenly retirement account. In Japan in 1945, Eric was given the privileged opportunity of release from his prisoner of war camp; Eric gave his place to a pregnant woman. That was a hefty deposit into his account.[1]

Rev. Pat Johnson of Long Island, a wife and mother of two children, had a dream to invest herself in God's kingdom work. God led Pat to leave her teaching position, to devote more time to her special needs son. While continuing her women's ministry at church, God gave her a desire to begin a new work for women on Long Island.

Pat, for four years, with her hubby alongside, prayed and did what she could to start a safe house for women. Through people and a series of events, God began to open doors to purchase a two-family home. God supernaturally worked through the maze of bureaucracy and red tape.

Meanwhile, God's people and her church, Point Lookout Community Church, caught the dream. They began to invest their prayers, time, expertise, and money to bring it to pass.

After months of fixing, replacing, painting, and furnishing, *Ruby's Place* is open! Fourteen women who are recovering from addictions, are victims of abuse, or are transitioning from prison to life are under the loving, godly, and wise care of Reverend Pat Johnson.

She not only invested in these women, but into her burgeoning retirement account, as have all who came alongside to make it happen!

When you invest yourself and your labors here, sometimes you may be disappointed. But, God is keeping accounts, and your labor will never be in vain. You will reap one day if you faint not (1 Corinthians 15:58; Galatians 6:9).

PRAYER: *Dear Lord, thank You that our labor for You is never in vain. Show me where to put my hand to the plow and then not to look back. I know my reward is You and from You, and will be waiting for me when I come home. Amen.*

Make it yours: Look at where you're putting your time and efforts and weigh it in the light of eternity. Are there any changes you have to make?

The Best Is Yet to Come

NOW THE DWELLING OF GOD IS WITH MEN,
AND HE WILL LIVE WITH THEM. THEY WILL BE HIS PEOPLE, AND
GOD HIMSELF WILL BE WITH THEM AND BE THEIR GOD.

Revelation 21:3

The travel ads and brochures always show the best of where we want to travel. From there it all goes downhill. However, our forever-vacation preview is a pale taste of the awesome wonder awaiting—and it gets even better!

Our heavenly package comes with a divine wedding feast that's all-inclusive. It's bigger and better than Donald Trump's latest nuptials, for it's Jesus' wedding feast for His beloved bride—you!

The apostle Paul had a glimpse of heaven and was speechless; John on Patmos fell as dead! (2 Corinthians 12:4; Revelation 1:17).

In the movie *Enchanted*[1], Princess Giselle is banished

to where there are no happy endings. True, life doesn't always give happy endings; nonetheless, with the Lord Jesus Christ, there's *always* a happy ending! We'll live forever with Him, surrounded by His love and glory; nevermore will there be pain, sorrow, tears, or death. It can't get any better! (Revelation 21:3–4).

Every religion has a concept of heaven, for God has put eternity in our hearts. Even as a child of a nonreligious family, I was fascinated by the idea of heaven and wanted to go. In the movie *Imitation of Life*[2] I was enthralled when I saw an old time southern funeral procession. The people walked behind the funeral carriage, singing and playing banjos as if it were a party. I was young and knew nothing about heaven, but, this made sense. If you really believed someone was going to heaven—it'd be a celebration for them. Happily, I eventually found the Bible agreed with my childlike theology.

The fierce tribe of warriors, the Waodoni Indians of Ecuador, tell the story of when they speared to death five missionaries, how they saw supernatural beings in the trees, singing beautiful music (they later found out that they were angels).[3]

My friend, Sue Henke, remembers at her father's home-going, that he heard the "Hallelujah Chorus." What a way to go home—and that's just a taste of what's waiting for us.

We're sojourners traveling home. The road before us

was stained red by His blood, turned bright yellow by His glory; then He paved it with pure joy for us to enjoy the journey home.

We will get there—where we'll sing heaven's song, "You are worthy, our Lord and God, to receive glory and honor and power" (Revelation 4:11).

He's put in your reservations; there's a table waiting!

Whatever's on your road today, turn your eyes heavenward and you'll see Him at the top of the ladder. Listen and hear His sweet love song to you, "It's for this you were created. It's for this I died. Enjoy the journey home—I have indeed saved the best for last for you!"

PRAYER: *Father, thank You for the promise and hope of heaven, where there's no disappointment. Help me live a life worthy of eternity. May I walk the way of joy with You till then. Amen.*

Make it yours: Tell someone about your hope of heaven, and let them know how they can put in a reservation. There is *always* room for one more.

Which Door?

I AM THE GATE [DOOR];
WHOEVER ENTERS THROUGH ME WILL
BE SAVED. HE WILL COME IN AND
GO OUT, AND FIND PASTURE.

John 10:9

Let's Make a Deal has been a popular TV game show since 1972. If the contestant makes it to the end, the announcer says, "Which door will it be?" There are three closed doors—one with the big prize behind. The show is great fun, and the contestants go home with a prize or cash. However, which door they choose isn't a matter of life or death.

Yet, everyone is faced with doors of opportunity throughout life—in marriage, a job, a move, or other situations. Sometimes the decision not only changes our life, but the lives of others.

However, there's one door that not only changes your life on this earth—but will affect your eternal destiny: It's the door of salvation.

I was twenty-seven before I heard that the way of salvation involved more than just being good. I was living the normal merry-go-round life of a wife and mother of two. Except it wasn't so merry sometimes.

I put myself under such pressure, even a simple phone ringing sent me for the bottle of tranquilizers. Then the unexpected death of my parents shook my already unsteady world.

Besides my deep grief, I now had big questions. *What happens when you die? What is life all about?* I tried going back to my childhood church whose hypocrisy had years ago turned me off of religion. They had no answers for me. Seeking peace and answers, I increased the speed of my merry-go-round.

God, being so merciful, pursued me until I found Him. He sent Donna Falta into my life. Through her love and prayers, she led me to the doorway of salvation.

She gave me a Bible and patiently answered my myriad of questions. I learned I couldn't work my sin away; I couldn't do enough good works to get to heaven. It was Jesus Christ, the Son of God, who had already earned my way for me (Romans 5:8). Donna told me even if I'd been the only one, He loved me enough to die just for me!

No words can describe what happened in my life once I chose to go through the open door of salvation.

God gave me true peace and joy, and a love for Him and His Word.

No matter what life has brought, no matter which doors I have chosen, I have weathered it—for He is the source of my peace and joy. While I didn't become instantly perfect, He began a gentle work that is still going on.

Each day is indeed an adventure with Him—and it keeps getting better.

"For God so loved the world that he gave his one and only Son, that whoever believes in him shall not perish but have eternal life" (John 3:16).

PRAYER: *Thank You Father, for Your Son Jesus Christ who died, was buried, and rose again for my sins. I come by faith and ask You to forgive me. I surrender myself to You, and thank You for coming into my life. I believe Your promises are true, and I am now Your child by faith. Amen. (If you know the Lord, thank Him again for His precious gift of salvation.)*

Make it yours: If you have prayed this prayer for the first time, tell someone. I'd love to hear from you via email: ComeBestYet@aol.com or through my website: http://franfernandezministry.spaces.live.com/. Look for a Bible-believing, preaching church and start attending faithfully. Read the Word daily and obey it.

If you know the Lord, ask Him for someone with whom you can share your testimony today, or soon.

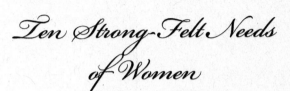

Ten Strong-Felt Needs of Women

Extreme Living

Knowing God

Glad Serving

Spirit Living

Living Faith

Worry-Free Living

God Cares

In His Image

Living Worship

Power Living

Notes

Chapter 1: Taking Your Mountains

Page 16: www.evamarieeverson.com

Page 16: Eva Marie Everson and Linda Evans Shepherd, *The Potluck Club* (Grand Rapids, Mich.: Revell, 2005), 382. *www.potluck.com.*

Chapter 2: God, Can You Help Me?

Page 21: Rick Weinberg, "94: Derek and dad finish Olympic 400 together," ESPN Counts Down the 100 Most Memorable Moments of the Past 25 Years, *ESPN.com: sports.espn.go.com/espn/espn25/ story?page=moments/94.*

Chapter 14: The Power of Joy

Page 55: Norman Cousins, *Anatomy of an Illness* (New York: Norton, 2005).

Chapter 16: Serve with Gladness

Page 61: E. Cobham Brewer and John Ayto, *Brewer's Dictionary of Phrase and Fable*, 17th ed. (London: Cassell Reference, 2007).

Chapter 17: Yes, You Can!

Page 64: Watty Piper, *The Little Engine That Could* (New York: Platt & Munk, 1930).

Page 66: June Vilandy, "Body Makeovers: Getting Younger at 62!" *Prevention* (April 1995): 122.

Chapter 21: Me, Lord?

Page 77: Mike Vasilinda, "Zach Bonner Walks 280 Miles for Homeless," November 26, 2007. *Capitol News Service. www.flanews.com/?p=1365.*

Chapter 30: Red Hot Prayers

Page 104: D. James Kennedy, PhD, Knox Theological Seminary Convocation Address, vol. 2, no. 3, *The Knox News*, September 2005.

Chapter 31: Delighting in His Word

Page 106: Russel Ash, *The Top 10 of Everything 1997* (New York: DK Publishing, 1997), 112–13.

Chapter 34: Hospital for Broken Hearts

Page 116: Don Piper with Cecil Murphey, *90 Minutes in Heaven* (Grand Rapids, Mich.: Revell, 2007).

Page 117: The Imperials, "Praise the Lord," *Classic Hits: Gospel Legacy Series: The Imperials: Through the Years*, New Haven, 2006.

Chapter 35: Yellow Mind-Set

Page 120: *Newsday*, sec. G, January 6, 2008.

Chapter 36: Setting Your GPS

Page 123: Patricia Willems, "Lives a Life of Service," *Reminisce Extra* (January 2008): 57.

Chapter 37: God Is for Me?

Page 125: *Ray* (Hollywood: Universal Studios Home Entertainment, 2004).

Chapter 44: I'm Creative?

Page 148: *www.essortment.com/all/informationong_ooc.htm*.

Page 148: Anita Palmer, "Mobile Blessings," *World Magazine*, vol. 23, no. 10, May 17, 2008.

Chapter 47: Evergreen Faith

Page 157: "Life Etc.," *AARP* September/October 2007, 88.

Chapter 48: The Real You

Page 161: Joseph P. Lash and Trude Lash, *Helen and Teacher: The Story of Helen Keller and Anne Sullivan Macy*, Radcliffe Biography Series (Cambridge: Da Capo Press, 1997).

Chapter 50: Power of One

Page 166: *The Legacy of George Washington Carver*, Iowa State University Library Special Collections Dept., *www.lib.iastate.edu/spcl/gwc/bio.html* (1998; revised March 2007).

Page 167: See en.wikipedia.org/wiki/Dream_Center; www.dreamcenter.org/.

Chapter 51: High Stepping in the Spirit

Page 169: Westminster Catechism, Question one.

Chapter 52: Thanksgiving Surround

Page 172: Special edition DVD "Life without Limbs," *www.lifewithoutlimbs.org*.

Chapter 53: More Than a Conqueror?

Page 175: See *www.auschwitz.dk/kolbe.htm*.

Chapter 55: While You Wait

Page 181: Mark Galli and Ted Olsen, ed., *131 Christians Everyone Should Know* (Nashville: Broadman & Holman, 2000).

Chapter 56: The Worthy Walk

Page 183: *www.thefreedictionary.com/noblesse+oblige*.

Page 184: Ruth Bell Graham, "Giants Among Us," *Decision Magazine* (December 2007).

Chapter 58: Investment Portfolio

Page 190: Eric Liddell Biography, *=www.telegraph.co.uk/sport/othersports/olympics/2436938/Eric-Liddell's-Story-to-set-Chinese-hearts-racing.html*.

Chapter 59: The Best Is Yet to Come

Page 192: *Enchanted* (Burbank, Calif.: Walt Disney, 2007).

Page 193: Fannie Hurst, *Imitation of Life 1934/1959* (New York: Harper & Brothers, 1933).

Page 193: *End of the Spear* (Los Angeles: 20th Century Fox, 2005).